THE
DNA
OF
GOD?

THE
DNA
OF
GOD?

Leoncio A.
Garza-Valdes

Berkley Books, New York

A Berkley Book
Published by The Berkley Publishing Group
A division of Penguin Putnam Inc.
375 Hudson Street
New York, New York 10014

Published by arrangement with Doubleday, a division of Doubleday Broadway
Publishing Group, a division of Random House, Inc.

PRINTING HISTORY
Doubleday hardcover edition / March 1999
Berkley trade paperback edition / June 2001

The Penguin Putnam Inc. world Wide Web site address is
www.penguinputnam.com

Library of Congress Cataloging-in-Publication Data

Garza-Valdes, Leoncio A.
The DNA of God? / Leoncio A. Garza-Valdes.
p. cm.
Originally published: New York : Doubleday, 1999.
Includes bibliographical references.
ISBN 0-425-17666-5
1. Holy Shroud.   I. Title.

BT587.S4 G37 2001
232.96′6—dc21
00-066750

PRINTED IN THE UNITED STATES OF AMERICA

10 9 8 7 6 5 4 3 2 1

To the memory of
FATHER FAUSTINO CERVANTES IBARROLA
December 5, 1917–January 20, 1995

CONTENTS

Acknowledgments • *ix*

Preface • *A Theological Note* • *xi*

Introduction • *1*

Chapter 1 • THE SHROUD—MY FIRST CONFRONTATION • *5*

Chapter 2 • THE FAKE THAT WAS NOT A FAKE • *12*

Chapter 3 • "HANDS-ON" WITH A PIECE OF THE SHROUD • *21*

Chapter 4 • "ARRIVEDERCI ROMA" • *29*

Chapter 5 • THE BACTERIA ARE ALIVE! • *33*

Chapter 6 • DNA IN THE BLOOD . . . • *38*

Chapter 7 • THE REDATING THAT WENT WRONG • *47*

Chapter 8 • HOW WAS THE IMAGE FORMED? • *55*

Chapter 9 • "KNIGHTS OF THE ROUND TABLE" • *60*

Chapter 10 • PROBLEMS WITH MUMMIES . . . • *67*

Chapter 11 • EVEN MORE PROBLEMS WITH

CARDINALS . . . • *73*

Chapter 12 • THE SWAN SONG • *78*

Chapter 13 • THE OAK OF GOLGOTHA • *83*

Chapter 14 • HIS HOLINESS JOHN PAUL II • *86*

Chapter 15 • LOOKING TO THE FUTURE • *92*

Appendix A • ANATOMY, BLOOD, AND DNA ON

THE SHROUD • *99*

Appendix B • A NATURALLY PLASTICIZED TEXTILE • *120*

Appendix C • THE OFFICIAL SHROUD PHOTOGRAPHS • *139*

Appendix D • AN ACCELERATOR-BASED MASS SPECTROMETRY

(H. GOVE) • *153*

Appendix E • THE CARBON DATING OF THE SHROUD OF

TURIN • *160*

Appendix F • THE TRUE CROSS • *187*

Notes for Appendices • *193*

Bibliography • *199*

ACKNOWLEDGMENTS

VATICAN CITY
    His Holiness John Paul II
    Bishop James Harvey
    Mons. Paolo De Nicolo
    Brother John Baldwin

TURIN
    Luigi Gonella
    Giovanni Riggi di Numana
    Professor Franco A. Testore

MICROBIOLOGY AT SANTA ROSA HOSPITAL,
SAN ANTONIO
    Adolphus Smith
    Teresa S. Widish
    Vicky A. Fitzhugh
    Victor Saldivar

MICROBIOLOGY AT DSM, BRAUNSCHWEIG
    Brian J. Tindall

MICROBIOLOGY AT TECHNICAL UNIVERSITY, MUNICH
    Karl H. Schleifer

INDUSTRIAL MICROBIOLOGY AT WAGENINGEN,
HOLLAND
  Gerrit Eggink

PHYSICS
  Harry E. Gove

CENTER FOR ADVANCED DNA TECHNOLOGY,
SAN ANTONIO
  Victor V. Tryon
  Nancy Mitchell Tryon

ANTHROPOLOGY, UNIVERSITY OF TEXAS AT AUSTIN
  Brian Stross

THEOLOGY, ST. MARY'S UNIVERSITY, SAN ANTONIO
  Father John A. Leies, Ph.D.

FIVE REVIEWERS OF THE FOURTH DRAFT
  Ann Guthrie
  Martha Magaly Huther
  Ylda Isabel Huther
  Jorge Martinez-Prieto
  Carole Slade

DOUBLEDAY EDITORIAL DEPARTMENT
  Trace Murphy

PREFACE

A THEOLOGICAL NOTE

The title of the book is provocative: *The DNA of God?* To some people it may seem irreligious or heretical or the attempt at a marketing ploy. Yet the title can be theologically defended.

In the first centuries of Christianity, the Church faced numerous efforts to explain the nature of Jesus of Nazareth, some of which were judged erroneous or misleading or dangerous. In the midst of examining the Christological questions, the Church developed a clear, official position: Jesus was both God and man, his nature as a human being was "hypostatically" joined to the divinity, he was of the same substance as God, at no time of his existence was he not God, and so on.

The issue of Jesus' nature came to the forefront in discussions concerning the relationship of Mary of Nazareth, his mother, to Jesus, her son. The title "Mother of God" was used by many Christians in reference to Mary. But serious objections to that usage were raised by others.

At a Council of Ephesus in A.D. 431, the Christian Church solemnly proclaimed its belief: Mary rightly could be called not only the Mother of Jesus but also the Mother of God. At no time was Jesus not God. In becoming the mother of Jesus, she was by that very fact the mother of God.

It is then theologically true that whatever pertains to Jesus pertains to God: the body of Jesus can be said to be the body of God; the words of Jesus, the words of God; the blood of Jesus, the blood of God; and the components of the blood of Jesus—the DNA, for example—can truly be said to be that of God.

It has not been proven that the man who was covered by the Shroud of Turin was Jesus of Nazareth. The question mark in the title indicates the uncertainty. But if it is the real Shroud of Jesus, then the bloodstains on it—and their DNA—are God's.

—REV. JOHN A. LEIES, S.M., S.T.D.,
St. Mary's University, San Antonio, Texas

THE
DNA
OF
GOD?

INTRODUCTION

THE SCIENTIFIC STUDY OF ANCIENT ARTIFACTS, IN-cluding the Shroud of Turin, has taken me around the world, finding my way through unknown scientific territory and complicated political intrigues. The journey has been marked both by soaring exhilaration and by profound discouragement. But the moment that stays with me always, as a personal and professional turning point, is when I first saw and handled actual linen samples taken from the Shroud. I had long had an interest in it, deeply moved by the possibility that this piece of cloth was the one physical link to Jesus Christ remaining on the earth. But even beyond the personal involvement was my interest, as a medical doctor, in the Shroud itself. It was the high moment in a journey of scientific discovery that was to have profound implications.

Though it may sound strange, that journey has had little to do with faith—but everything to do with science. Many people acknowledge the authenticity of the Shroud of Turin as an "article of faith," an identification to be accepted on trust alone rather than on facts. In the same way that few people think it worthwhile to attempt to prove scientifically the divinity of Jesus of Nazareth, I doubt the possibility of proving that the Shroud of Turin is truly the burial cloth of Jesus. But we live in an age of skepticism and try to explain all phenomena according to scientific criteria.

Although I have deep feelings in matters of faith (including the Shroud itself), I am more comfortable with the demands of science when seeking the "truth." In fact, my entire professional life has been based on the scientific method. Research requires physical evidence; without it, the scientific method is useless. Accordingly, I am not about to offer judgment on a matter for which there is no evidence, that is, whether the Shroud is without doubt the burial cloth of Jesus, or whether the image on the Shroud was wrought through divine or supernatural means. I do not expect to lay to rest all the controversies that have surrounded the Shroud for centuries.

Yet even though I do not have answers for all these questions, I have gathered some extraordinary information—information that solves many of the mysteries of the Shroud and will have direct bearing for years to come on further study of the subject. Much of the physical evidence about the Shroud was never, until recently, studied with the aid of up-to-date scientific equipment and methods. Although some microscopic pieces of evidence raise further questions, I found them to offer insight into the Shroud's history. They helped me, and will undoubtedly be of use to scientists who will carry on the research in the years ahead.

The evidence I have found has broad implications. For example, my research has clarified many puzzles about the age of the Shroud, particularly the 1988 radiocarbon dating, whose proponents concluded that the Shroud does not date from the time of Jesus of Nazareth. I now know that this conclusion was mistaken, but the reasons were not apparent back in 1988.

I have discovered on the Shroud what I call a bioplastic coating, a type of clear encasing that is invisible to the unaided eye. Today, it looks to viewers like a shiny lamination, which is why some eyewitnesses say the Shroud has a surprising "surface sheen." It is not, however, a manmade coating; it is actually composed of millions of living microbiological organisms that have formed over time, somewhat like a coral reef. This is a natural process I had earlier noted while doing research on other ancient artifacts. When the scientists used carbon dating on Shroud samples in 1988, they did not realize that they were dating, as one entity, both the original ancient fabric and this living bioplastic coating. Their mistaken result was off by centuries. My conclusion, based on evidence I have gathered, is that the Shroud of Turin is not a medieval fake, as was suggested, but is quite possibly a relic of the time of Jesus of Nazareth.

Beyond that important finding, I have come upon other microscopic clues that are surprisingly consistent with the Gospel accounts of the death and burial of Jesus. I isolated bacteria that produce acetic acid (vinegar). Were they traces of the vinegar offered to Jesus on a sponge as he died on the cross? Infinitesimal splinters of hard wood (oak) were found near the occipital wound areas of the Man on the Shroud. Could these be actual pieces of the True Cross? And what about the blood remnants I found on the Shroud that contain human male DNA? Is this the DNA of Jesus and, by direct consequence, of God?

I offer my story to you, the reader, in the hope that you will share the wonder I felt with each of these discoveries. My hope is that the account will lead to a deeper recognition of the significance of this relic, as well as of the importance of further careful study of the secrets the Shroud contains.

On July 29, 1998, I gave a copy of this manuscript to His Holiness John Paul II directly during an audience at the Vatican. This moment will always be present in my mind.

Chapter I

THE
SHROUD—
MY FIRST
CONFRONTATION

T HERE IS NO ONE MOMENT IN MY LIFE WHEN I REMEM-
ber learning about the Shroud of Turin. Like many people, I
had been familiar with the name since I was a child. My first specific
recollections go back to the pictures of the Holy Face, photographs
from the negative plate of the Man on the Shroud that my mother, a
devout Catholic, had stored between the pages of her missal. The
mystery associated with the pictures filled me with a sense of wonder I
have held ever since. But I know now that even then I had questions
about what was seen in the relic.

Many years later, during a vacation in Italy, I went to visit St.
John the Baptist Cathedral in Turin, and though the Shroud itself was
not on view, there was displayed a full-size transparency of it. I had
not come with high expectations; I thought I would see nothing more
than an old dusty remainder from the past. Yet even though the life-
size image was only a facsimile, I was stunned by what I saw, and my
childhood wonder grew into profound awe. Having expected to see
an artifact of history, I now felt that I was looking at an imprint of
history, at once so distant yet so familiar.

The Shroud seemed to me much more relevant, and I was eager to look into the science behind it, keeping in mind my experience as a physician and a professor of microbiology, as well as my enthusiasm for archaeology. At this stage my curiosity had more to do with a hobby, not a vocation. But I had followed the latest research; there was much to learn.

Because the Shroud of Turin has been the object of devout attention for so many centuries, a special term was devised to refer to those people who have dedicated themselves to its study. They are called "Sindonologists," which comes from the Greek term *sindon,* which means "garment" or "sheet." These Shroudies, as they are sometimes called, are always eager for fresh information that may shed light on the mysteries of the Shroud. I think, perhaps, they hope that each bit of information will help to prove the Shroud's authenticity. Since I did not have such a personal stake in the Shroud, I was spared the shock that many enthusiasts had on October 13, 1988, when it was announced, in Turin and in London, that the Shroud had been found to date from between 1260 and 1390 and must therefore be a medieval fake.

Although this was treated as important news, printed on front pages around the world, the announcement did not come as a surprise to me. I knew that doubts about the Shroud's authenticity had been expressed over the centuries. In 1389, in fact, a French clergyman, Bishop Pierre d'Arcis, wrote, of the Shroud, then being exhibited in the small French village of Lirey, that he had learned it was "a work of human skill, and not divinely wrought or bestowed." Similar doubts were voiced over the years, but in May 1898 they were largely dispelled when an Italian councilor, Secondo Pia, took the first official photograph of the cloth. To everyone's surprise, the negative plate revealed a startlingly lifelike "photograph," which had been invisible to the human eye until then.

As photography advanced, a picture taken in the 1930s confirmed that the image on the negative plate was neither an accident nor a sham. And with the aid of these better photographs, physicians around the world—Dr. Pierre Barbet in France, Dr. David Willis in England, Dr. Hermann Moedder in Germany, Dr. Judica-Cordiglia in Italy, Dr. Robert Bucklin in the United States, and others—began a close study of the physiognomy of the person pictured on the Shroud. They became convinced that the image was that of someone who had been crucified in the same manner as Jesus of Nazareth. Anatomically and physiologically, the image was too convincing to be the handiwork of a medieval artist.

On this point it is helpful to remember that the idea of a "realistic"-looking image is different today from what it was in the Middle Ages. Not until Leonardo da Vinci, in the fifteenth century, did post-Classical artists begin to pay attention to the details of human anatomy. I recalled, too, that the trees in the paintings of Giotto, the Florentine painter of the thirteenth century, the same period in which carbon dating placed the Shroud, were praised by his contemporaries for their realism. Yet when we look at these pictures today, they are more likely to remind us of pieces of broccoli than of trees. Our contemporary idea of a lifelike image has been significantly shaped by photographic and electronic imaging. So it is surely impressive that we—especially physicians—can see on the Shroud an impeccably realistic image of a human figure.

More support for the Shroud's authenticity appeared during the 1970s, when the Swiss criminologist Dr. Max Frei discovered and identified pollen grains in the dust on the Shroud. The pollen was from plants unique to the Holy Land and to Turkey, proving that the Shroud had at some time been exposed to the air in these places. Reinforcement came in 1978, when the American STURP (Shroud of Turin Research Project), comprising about thirty scientists from the Los Alamos National Scientific Laboratory, the Air Force Weapons Laboratory, the Jet Propulsion Laboratory, and other American scientific institutions, carried out a five-day close examination of the Shroud of Turin. Their tests included microscopy, infra-red spectroscopy, X-radiography, and the examination of over thirty samples, from both image and blank areas, collected on small strips of specially formulated sticky tape. (Little did I know that years later I would be allowed to study one of the tape samples of a suspected bloodstain.) In their subsequent published reports, the STURP scientists concluded that the Shroud's image was not paint but some kind of degradation of the cellulose (oxidative dehydration), a chemical reaction caused by the release of energy at the time of the Resurrection. (This was later proved wrong by my research.) They further confirmed that the marks the faithful had for many years identified as bloodstains—though detractors said they were merely some sort of pigment—had indeed been made by blood.

Also in 1978 the English writer Ian Wilson identified the Shroud as a historically known cloth that had been kept in the Turkish city of Edessa (modern-day Urfa), then in Constantinople between 944 until its disappearance in 1204. This seemed consistent with the pollen findings, and partly explained where the Shroud had been before Bishop d'Arcis noted its appearance in the village of Lirey in the late fourteenth century.

These findings seemed to support the idea that the Shroud truly was a sort of portrait of Jesus' resurrection—a divine gift to the materialism of the times in which we live. There was, however, one further scientific test that had not yet been carried out, one that could show more accurately whether the Shroud does or does not date from the time of Jesus. This was radiocarbon dating, the "atomic clock" method of placing in time ancient objects of organic origin, such as wood, linen, and bone, by determining the extent to which they have lost their radioactive carbon 14, the carbon atom that every living thing takes in during its lifespan. When an organism dies, its carbon 14 begins to decay at a predictable rate. It is difficult to be completely accurate in dating objects of recent origin, since there can be wide variations in the presence of carbon 14 soon after death. But when you go back beyond a thousand years, the presence is more stable and the dating, therefore, more reliable.

Archaeologists and anthropologists have greatly benefited from this scientific technique, which has expanded and deepened our understanding of unrecorded history. Some objects are more easy to date than others. For example, pieces of charcoal, perhaps from an ancient fireplace, provide consistent dating results; pieces of bone, however, have proved less certain. Generally, plant material is more reliable, and this would surely be true of the flax plant, the source of the fibers for linen. Ever since the availability of the carbon-dating process, people have hoped to apply it to the Shroud, but permission was refused, because it would have required a piece of linen as big as a pocket handkerchief to be cut from the cloth. What's more, for an object to be carbon-dated, it must be incinerated, so there is no way to preserve the piece after it has been cut away. King Umberto of Italy, who owned the Shroud in the 1970s, when the STURP research was done, was advised that this was too great a sacrifice. Then, in the late 1970s, Professor Harry Gove, director of the Nuclear Structure Research Laboratory at the University of Rochester, in New York State, together with colleagues, developed a new method of carbon dating called accelerator mass spectroscopy, or AMS. Instead of requiring a large piece of fabric, this method could use a sample no bigger than a postage stamp. If such a fragment of material was considered an acceptable sacrifice by those who guarded the Shroud, there was the possibility of determining the date of its creation, within seventy to a hundred years.

But in 1983, before King Umberto could reach a decision, he died. He had bequeathed the Shroud to the Pope and his successors in perpetuity, with the understanding that it would stay in Turin. Not long after, the Vatican agreed to have Gove's AMS carbon-dating method applied to the Shroud. Archbishop Cardinal Ballestrero of Turin, the Shroud's custodian on behalf of the Pope, appointed three radiocarbon-dating laboratories to take part: one at the University of Oxford, England, one at the University of Zürich, Switzerland, and one at the University of Arizona at Tucson. Representatives of each institution were invited to Turin. On April 21, 1988, the Shroud was brought out and, in their presence, had a portion cut off and divided among the scientists, who took the pieces back to their laboratories. Extra pieces were set aside in case there was a later need for further samples.

Six months later came an announcement that upset the Shroudies. On October 13, 1988, at nearly simultaneous conferences in Turin and London, the results of the three laboratories were released. In London the press conference, held at the British Museum, was headed by the museum's Dr. Michael Tite, who had been the overall supervisor of all three research teams. He was joined by Oxford's Professor Edward Hall and by Dr. Robert Hedges, the chief Oxford technician. Behind them on a blackboard someone had triumphantly chalked, in very large letters, 1260–1390!

As the three men explained, the datings independently arrived at by all three laboratories were so similar as to indicate, with a certainty close to 95 percent, that the Shroud's flax had been cut down to be made into linen sometime between these dates.

As might have been expected, some devotees tried to suggest that there had been a switching of samples, inadvertent or otherwise. Several books have been written to explore this idea. However, I believe that the scientists who worked on the carbon dating were honest men and good scientists who carried out their procedures as thoroughly as could be done at the time.

Then in London, on February 14, 1989, Professor Edward Hall gave a public lecture, sponsored by the British Museum Society, which he entitled "The Turin Shroud—A Lesson in Self-Persuasion." His purpose was to counter the doubts of anyone who questioned the carbon-dating findings. He explained that his laboratory carried out a thousand carbon datings a year, and no one had found fault with their conclusions. With regard to the possibility of some contamination having affected the result of the Shroud's test, he said that both his laboratory and the two others had used special solvents to preclude any such error. Twenty percent of the sample had been dissolved by this process. There would have had to be a "ridiculous" 60 percent level of modern contamination for a first-century Shroud to be dated as belonging to the Middle Ages. Overall, he said, he would have been amazed if even a 1 percent level of contamination had been left.

I would never have guessed that I, a pediatrician who grew up in Monterrey, Mexico, would be called on to prove that this distinguished scientist was wrong. I had no idea that the inquiries I was about to make, in a completely different area of interest, would cast a different light on the mystery of the Shroud.

THE FAKE
THAT WAS NOT
A FAKE

T HE MOST IMPORTANT ASPECT OF MY INVESTIGATIONS into the Shroud developed from a personal interest I would never have associated with it: my studies of ancient Maya culture. As much as I love my work in medicine and microbiology, I have found much satisfaction, over the past forty years, in my investigations of the archaeology of the ancient Maya people. Classic Maya culture flourished between A.D. 200 and 900 in an area known as Mesoamerica, the tropical lowlands of Guatemala, southeast Mexico, Belize, Honduras, and El Salvador. The period between 1000 B.C. and A.D. 200 is known as the pre-Classic period, and the period between A.D. 900 and 1500, the post-Classic. Maya civilization enriched human history with its architecture, knowledge of astronomy, and a highly developed civic structure. My interest in Maya archaeology was sparked when I was in elementary school, in the early 1950s, and saw the movie *El Pueblo del Sol* (The People of the Sun), the story of Alfonso Caso, an archaeologist who worked on a Zapotec tomb at Monte Alban where jade artifacts were discovered. The jade carvings endowed the Mesoamerican rulers with shamanic powers. For me, a ten-year-old boy hungry for adventure, the jades represented a beautiful, dangerous, and thrilling past I wanted to know more about. The history surrounding them was fascinating; they seemed to have secrets locked within them about the people who had owned them, the tragedies and adventures they had witnessed. I liked to imagine peering back through time to unlock those secrets.

Jade was the most prized material of the Mesoamericans, considered even more valuable than gold. Those materials which a culture most prizes inevitably become associated with nonmaterial values. For example, an archaeologist in the thirty-first century, learning of the value we today place on gold, would rightly assume that a gold wedding band must have symbolized an abstract idea we also deemed valuable. So it is that we can look at Maya jades and gain some understanding of the Maya view of the world and what they believed to be important, perhaps sacred.

The enthusiasm initiated by the story of Alfonso Caso became more compelling later, when I saw some of these ancient jades at the National Museum of Anthropology in Mexico City. I was awed by their beauty and their luster, and I remember marveling that they had retained such a polish over the thousand years and more since they were made.

Though I played with the idea of becoming an archaeologist adventurer (*a là* Indiana Jones), my desire for a more practical life won out, and when I was in college, I decided to become a doctor. Along with my medical studies, I pursued an interest in microbiology. In 1960, in my third year at medical school, I became absorbed by the studies of biochemistry, microbiology, and the metabolic pathways of bacteria. I remember a classmate saying that I was the only person he knew who could reach *ecstasy* by talking about metabolic pathways! It did indeed become something of a passion—and a profitable passion, too, because thirty-five years later I was to use these pathways to help explain the anomalies in the dating of the Turin Shroud.

Through all this, though, my interest in jades remained, as I completed my medical degree and established a private practice as a pediatrician and pediatric cardiologist. In my practice, I remained active in various types of research, much of it related to pediatrics and cardiology. I reported to the American College of Cardiology my findings concerning a hereditary condition that can cause certain children to develop a ventricular fibrillation that may kill them if they take strong medicines or have too much exercise. To the American Academy of Pediatrics I reported on the mechanism of supraventricular tachycardia by repetitive reciprocation; that is, a rapid heart rate produced by an anomaly in impulse conduction that may send the heart impulses back from the ventricles to the upper chambers and back again to the ventricles, establishing a vicious cycle. These findings were published in 1969 in *The American Journal of Cardiology* and, in 1970, in *Circulation*.

Between 1980 and 1984, I applied my medical experience to my studies for an M.A. in anthropology, with an emphasis in archaeometry, the scientific discipline of dating ancient artifacts. My knowledge of chemistry was particularly useful to these studies, which rekindled my enthusiasm for Maya jades. I decided to focus on them, and therefore studied geology and mineralogy so that I would be able to recognize the composition of different rocks. I also learned optical mineralogy, the study, with an optical microscope, of the minerals that form a rock, and geochemistry, the analysis of its chemical composition. I also studied gemology and felt sufficiently qualified to start doing field work. One of my best friends was Dr. George Harlow, Curator of Minerals and Gems at the American Museum of Natural History, and during the mid-1980s he and I made three trips into the jungles of Guatemala to study the geology of the area. We stayed in area villages and each day drove a truck into the jungle to find the jades at riverbeds and outcrops in the places where these metamorphic rocks are formed, the fault zones, which undergo intense geologic activity. At the riverbeds, all we had to do was look around to find the rocks we were seeking, and at the large outcrops we needed to do only superficial digging.

What I noticed immediately was the absence of the beautiful luster I had seen years earlier on the museum pieces. These natural, rough pieces of jade had secondary weathering at their surface, changes that intrigued me so much that I brought samples to my laboratory in San Antonio to study their chemical make-up.

As they age, many rocks develop a black coating, often referred to as a varnish (rock varnish, desert varnish, biogenic varnish). Although I studied these secondary formations on the jades, I could not explain all the changes on the *patina,* but only the secondary mineral formations, such as the change of pyroxene and feldspars into kaolin and smectite. The origin of my beautiful luster remained a mystery.

I still didn't know what to make of the gloss on my carved jades, but assumed that the luster was the product of polishing by the carver. Yet I knew that the environment was also involved, because I found on the Maya jades the presence of blood, roots, and phytoliths, together with the mineral changes that could have happened only over the course of centuries. It was not until later, around 1983, that I realized that the key to understanding the problem lay in microbiology.

When I was twenty-three, I had a stroke of good fortune. As I sought out experts who could expand my knowledge of Maya artifacts, I met Professor A. Rubio, from Monterrey, who was knowledgeable about the subject and had access to some beautiful pieces. His personal collection of jades, which I later named the Ahaw Collection, comprised carved green rocks of different mineral composition, the most important of which were some true jadeitites (rocks with jadeite as the principal mineral) and some albitites (rocks with albite as the principal mineral). I admired these pieces because of their beautiful carvings and their luster, and when Professor Rubio, on his retirement in 1970, decided to sell some of the pieces, I was lucky enough to be able to buy two: the Ahaw Pectoral and the Itzamna Tun, carved gems that were used by the Maya shaman, the king, to carry out his powers of magic. These were the first pieces in my own Maya artifact collection, later to be augmented by purchases from Sotheby's in New York.

Fate took a hand in 1983, when I reported on my Ahaw Pectoral to the Society for American Archaeology. The rock, green jasper composed mostly of fine-grained quartz, is an emerald-green carved gem of five pieces, originally held together by cotton string threaded through twenty perforations. Twelve of the holes still bear traces of fibrous elements of twisted yarn, and thousands of opaline bodies, known as phytoliths, were found deposited at the pectoral's surface that was not repolished. According to A. Piperno, "Phytoliths are particles of hydrated silica formed in the cells of living plants that are liberated from the cells upon death and decay of the plants." Some of these phytoliths were dumbbells with saddle-shaped structures from the tropical rain forest, the herbaceous bamboo *Streptochaeta sodiroana*. This herbaceous bamboo has a narrow distribution at the tropical rain forest of southeastern Guatemala, the southern part of Belize, and the northern part of Honduras in Mesoamerica, indicating the probable area of provenience of the pectoral. The iconography and technology date the piece to the Late Classic Maya Period. An ancient Olmec stone carving, known as the La Venta Altar 4, indicates that this pectoral was probably worn by a Maya king around his neck, as the Olmec ruler shown in Altar 4 wore his. The pectoral represented the ruler's power but was more than just a symbol. It was meant to signify the portal between this world and that of the ruler's ancestors, the connotation was that the ruler himself could travel through the portal to the other world and communicate with his ancestors, should he so choose.

Although the exact provenance of the piece was unknown, two Mesoamerican archaeologists in Texas concluded in 1978 that the Ahaw Pectoral was one of the most important pre-Columbian artifacts known, in part because of its iconography, which transformed the ruler who wore it in the *axis mundi,* and in part because of its great beauty.

But in 1983, after I gave my report to the Society for American Archaeology, two pre-Columbian art connoisseurs from New York told me they believed that the Ahaw Pectoral was a fake, citing as the basis of the judgment the very sheen that has fascinated me. Nonetheless, they graciously offered to buy both the Ahaw Pectoral and the Itzamna Tun for their collection of fakes, an offer I had no reservations about declining. Though I was hardly pleased by their assessment, I could understand their wariness. The world of ancient artifacts is indeed littered with fakes, and establishing an object's authenticity is not—and should not be—an easy process. It is necessary to study scientifically the surface of the piece and observe the evidence of how much time has passed since it was created. How has it reacted with the environment? In the case of my treasured jades, what could the glossy coat tell me about their history? The notion that my jades were not authentic was the spur I needed to carry out more substantive research on them. For my own peace of mind I had to find out whether the coating was the product of natural weathering over the centuries or of more recent origin.

Accordingly, I embarked on a series of tests, by thirteen different analytical methods, to study the Itzamna Tun, the Ahaw Pectoral, and four other ancient artifacts. The optical microscopy studies on the Itzamna Tun gave me the first clue to the natural origin of the luster; it could not have been made by man. I found millions of blue-green, gram-positive bacteria, which produced a pink pigment and also some fungi that varied from dark brown to black. Together, these made a yellowish "plastic coat," and because the gloss was formed by bacteria, I called it a "bioplastic coating."

From the standpoint of a microbiologist, it is a beautiful creation because of its chemical make-up, durability, and translucence. The composition of the plastic, I found, is a polyester, or PHA.

(Polyhydroxyalkanoate is similar to an acrylic.) Scanning electron microscopy showed that the coating on the Ahaw Pectoral was 20 micrometers thick. Under the electron microscope I was also able to discern tiny fragments of the cotton string that had held together the five pieces. When I removed them with a hypodermic needle, I discovered that they too were covered with fungi and bioplastic coating. Contemporary science can be highly sophisticated, but the most beautiful tests—and often the most compelling—are those which can be done very simply, as with the optical microscope. But modern technology took over when I needed to establish the composition of the patina. The coating was examined by infra-red spectroscopy performed by the Southwest Research Institute in San Antonio, an industrial analysis laboratory I had relied on for twenty years. The scrapings were stained with amido black, which is used to detect the presence of protein, and to my delight, the sample accepted the stain and showed the presence of organic deposits. As soon as this was evident, I knew I had solved the mystery of the luster, it was *organic,* not manmade.

ITZAMNA TUN

But the problem of the authenticity remained unanswered. For this aspect of the research, I drew on my knowledge of the likely history of the Itzamna Tun. The celt (a tool shaped like a chisel or ax head) is carved out of jade and is about 23 centimeters tall, 8 centimeters wide, and 5 centimeters deep. The front of the celt shows Itzamna, the god of the shamans and of medicine. From the back, it can be seen that it was fashioned in the shape of a penis, with three double perforations, indicating that it was used in conjunction with ritual bloodletting. (Of the different kinds of sacrifice common among the Maya, one called for the king to sacrifice his blood to the gods in the hope of a favorable return. The hoped-for result, often, was rain, essential for

crops and hence for the survival of the people.) There was no practical function for the Itzamna Tun; it was purely ritualistic and the jade
was probably kept on an altar in the Holy of Holies of the pyramid
temple. Only the king himself was allowed to enter this dark room.
Each Maya kingdom had a distinct celt, always regarded as being
sacred, embodying the very identity of the people. The word *tun* refers to both "stone" and to "the end of the year," and all Maya kings
would perform the same annual ritual to Itzamna at the close of each
year to ensure rain for the following year.

A few days of abstinence would be followed by the king's warm-
ing copal, the dried yellowish sap from trees of the genus *Bursera,*
which would create dense clouds of smoke the king would inhale. He
would then withdraw his penis from his clothing, cut it with a cere-
monial blade (bloodletter), and collect the blood in a small container,
sometimes made of paper formed from cactus. Half of the blood
would be carefully smeared by hand over the celt, and the rest would
be burned as an offering to Itzamna. In light of the likely history of
this kind of celt, it seemed sensible to test for the presence of blood on
the Itzamna Tun. If blood was present, I could have a sample of it
carbon dated. If the blood proved to be old, the authenticity of the
celt would also be established. I found several brown spots on the
celt's surface, between the grains of the stone, inside the eye cavities
of the carving, inside the mouth, and inside the perforations along the
back, and tested the deposits that were removed from the celt's right
eye socket. The optical microscope showed them to have a granular
crusty appearance and to have been laid down in the shape of a cross,
as they probably had been when applied by the kings during the ritual
smearing of the celt.

Further testing at the Santa Rosa Hospital and at the medical
examiner's office in San Antonio showed that these dark deposits
were definitely blood, definitely ancient, and definitely of human origin. The next step was to have the samples radio-carbon dated to
establish their exact age. So in 1991 I took the Itzamna Tun to the

radio-carbon dating facility at the University of Arizona, where I met Dr. Timothy Jull, one of the associates, who had coincidentally been part of the team that performed the 1988 dating of the Shroud of Turin.

The results of Dr. Jull's test, however, seemed strange. The radio-carbon age was 1535 years, plus or minus 240 years—giving it a range of dates from A.D. 240 to 690. These dates confirmed my conviction that the artifact was genuinely old and not a fraud, thus disproving the claims of the two New York "experts." On the other hand, the dates were more recent than what I had expected. The artistic styling of the Itzamna Tun indicated that it was several centuries older. The answer to the anomaly had to lie with the composition of the sample tested in Arizona. Perhaps something was mixed with the blood and threw off the dating. That something was surely the bioplastic coating, caused by the bacteria I had found when studying the samples microscopically.

And it was this conclusion that later came to mind when I was considering the Shroud of Turin.

Chapter 3

"HANDS-ON"
WITH A PIECE
OF THE SHROUD

M Y FIRST FORAYS INTO RESEARCH ON THE TURIN Shroud were a result of my meeting Dr. Alan Adler, Professor of Chemistry at Western Connecticut State University. In May 1987, I had organized a symposium in San Antonio entitled "Scientific Perspectives on the Problems of Art and Artifact Origins." Earlier, I had read *Report on the Shroud of Turin,* a book written by Dr. John Heller, who had worked with Alan Adler. As I carefully studied the photographs in the book, I found that they displayed a coating, and I was curious to get Adler's reaction to my findings on the bioplastic coating. I invited him to give a paper at the symposium on his work with the Shroud. This was a year before the carbon dating was done. Although Adler had not participated in STURP's testing of the Shroud of Turin, he took part in the group's research not long afterward. His involvement began when Dr. Ray Rodgers, a member of the STURP team, returned from Turin with several Mylar tapes he had applied to different areas of the Shroud. The plan was to determine what was on the surface of the linen and what might have caused the image.

The tapes were passed on to Dr. Walter McCrone, an optical microscopist in Chicago, in whose opinion the Shroud markings were a painting and the bloodlike stains were the pigments red ochre and vermillion. Samples of the tapes were also given to Dr. Adler and Dr. Heller, who completely disagreed with McCrone's claims. They believed that the Shroud stains were denatured, or partly destroyed, ancient blood, and, with a microspectrophotometer, were able to show the presence of hemoglobin (using the Soret absorption band). I had a long conversation with Dr. Adler at the 1987 symposium about the discrepancy between his findings and Dr. McCrone's, and I told him of my research on the blood on my Maya artifacts.

In April 1993, Adler was kind enough to send me a glass slide with a piece of Mylar tape on it. Under the tape were six microfibrils, and a "blood" sample 0.18 millimeters in diameter, taken from the blood of the left hand by Rodgers back in 1978. Apparently, Adler did not regard this as a particularly important sample, since the slide was broken, but for me it was an exciting first step into the mysteries of the Shroud. I examined the fibrils under an optical microscope and printed the photographs in my report of December 1993, "Bio-Plastic Coating on the Shroud of Turin: A Preliminary Report." But analysis of this sample showed that the blood itself had been completely replaced by fungi and bacteria. The PCR studies were negative; even if there had been human DNA there at one time, no sign of it remained.

When I first heard about the 1988 radiocarbon dating, I did not pay much attention to it; I was still focused primarily on the Maya celt. But I did hear about the findings, and they stayed in the back of my mind. Later, as I was on my way to deliver a paper at a conference on shamanism, it suddenly occurred to me that the discrepancy in the dating of the Itzamna Tun, which I believed was caused by the bioplastic coating, was analogous to the discrepancy in the dating of the Shroud. The cause might, in fact, be the same.

The best way to test my hypothesis, it seemed, was to go to Turin and try to study samples of the Shroud. I decided to seek guidance from someone who was familiar with Turin, so on my return from the shamanism conference I telephoned an old friend in Mexico City, Padre José Luis Guerrero. He had written a beautiful book about the Virgin of Guadalupe and the image of her that appeared on the cloak of Juan Diego, so I invited him to go with me to Turin. Unfortunately, he was too busy with the subject of Our Lady of Guadalupe, but he put me in touch with Father Faustino Cervantes Ibarrola, the spiritual director of the Mexican Center of Sindonology, who was delighted by my invitation. To him, my request seemed Divine Providence, since it happened to be the fiftieth anniversary of his ordination as a priest. He enthusiastically agreed to accompany me, and he drafted a fax in Italian to Cardinal Giovanni Saldarini, Archbishop of Turin, who in 1990 had replaced Cardinal Ballestrero. Father Cervantes gave an outline of my possible solution to the radiocarbon dating problem and requested that I be given access to the Shroud.

The fax was sent on April 26, 1993, and though he received no reply, we were undeterred, and boldly made our preparations to travel to Turin. It was a leap of faith, but we knew we had a highly plausible solution to the problem of the carbon dating. Perhaps it was as well that we did not know that a reply to the fax had in fact been drafted by Don Giuseppe Ghiberti, on Cardinal Saldarini's behalf, not granting us permission to study the Shroud! The fax, dated April 30, 1993, had been sent to the wrong fax number in Mexico City and was not received by Father Cervantes until after we returned from Turin.

On Saturday morning, May 15, 1993, Father Cervantes, my son Leoncio, and I flew from Newark, New Jersey, to Milan, where we arrived on Sunday. As we were buying train tickets for Turin, Father Cervantes' briefcase, containing his daily missal and other personal items, was stolen. My son was in charge of our equipment—a Nikon Optiphot microscope with a Nikon computerized camera, and an external fiberoptic illuminator to apply reflected light to samples to be studied with the microscope—and that, fortunately, was not stolen.

On our arrival in Turin, we telephoned Professor Luigi Gonella, who had been Cardinal Ballestrero's chief scientific adviser for the STURP testing and the radiocarbon dating. He agreed to meet us after we had been to Mass that afternoon at the Salesian Church of Don Bosco. The hospitable priests provided a room for our meeting with Gonella and allowed Father Cervantes to concelebrate Mass that evening.

Our first meeting with Gonella did not go smoothly. More than a little reserved, puffing on his pipe, Gonella did not seem to be paying attention to my description of the theory of the bioplastic coating. Indeed, he was completely skeptical. He said it was not plausible, because the coating would double the weight of the Shroud, and this was not the case. But since we did not know what the Shroud weighed two thousand years ago, I pointed out, it was impossible to know whether it had increased. I showed him some pictures from my study of the Maya jades alongside pictures published by the STURP group that appeared to show a coating. I explained that it was a real possibility that the type of coating present on ancient Maya artifacts was present on the Shroud; all I asked was the opportunity to study a segment of the Shroud. I did not ask to take away any material, just to examine it under an optical microscope. Unmoved, Gonella stated that it would be impossible to get permission to remove the Shroud from its casket. But after a further two hours of conversation, during which I elaborated on my work with the jades and my thoughts on the possible effects of the bioplastic coating, Gonella seemed to soften a little and agreed to talk to Cardinal Saldarini and inform us of the outcome.

In 1988, a sample of the Shroud had been divided among the radio-carbon laboratories for the dating tests. The cutting was done by Professor Giovanni Riggi di Numana, a Turin microanalyst, who we knew had close contact with both Luigi Gonella and Cardinal Balles-trero. The samples were weighed by Professor Franco A. Testore of the Turin Polytechnic University. Three pieces had been trimmed from the edge of the Shroud sample, which, Gonella said, Cardinal Ballestrero wanted him and Riggi to save for a later program of scientific research. Gonella—seeming to recognize that I had integrity as a scientist and had a worthy hypothesis to be explored—informed Riggi of my work, and Riggi called us at our hotel. When we met him that evening, we were surprised and relieved by his enthusiasm. Perhaps things had not gone so badly with Gonella, after all. Riggi arrived at our hotel about nine o'clock, and we wound up talking until two in the morning, with Father Cervantes translating from Spanish to Italian between us. Initially, it felt like a slow game of verbal Ping-Pong because of the language barrier. After many hours of questioning me vigorously, Riggi seemed convinced that my hypothesis was worth looking into and invited us to visit him later in the week.

We still, however, had to convince the Cardinal. When we went by the next day, Cardinal Saldarini did not receive us but instead sent out his secretary, Don Luciano Morello, to talk to us. Although he was friendly and spoke to us in English, we were soon interrupted when he received a phone call. Speaking in Italian to the person on the other end, he said, "I'll be finished with these people in five minutes." If we had been hopeful before, we now knew better. Immediately after hanging up the phone, he told us that the protocol for study of the Shroud was very long, and we were dismissed.

Since we were nearby, we visited the cathedral where the Shroud was housed. The cathedral was not as large as I had expected nor was the illumination good, but it gave me a sensation of peace. Behind the main altar was the beautiful Plexiglas fire- and bullet-proof box containing the silver reliquary, which in turn contained the Shroud. (This was the box that was destroyed on April 11, 1997, by the fireman Mario Trematore so that he could save the Shroud from the fire.) At one side of the altar was a full-size color transparency of the Shroud, the first of this kind that I had seen, and it was impressive.

The following day after lunch we went to the house of Giovanni Riggi. I was afraid that his enthusiasm might have waned. When we entered his library, we saw some packages that, we learned, he had taken from a personal safe deposit box at the bank. Inside one of them, he said, was the Petri dish containing three pieces of trimming from the edge of the Shroud. These were the 1988 samples he had told us about. The Petri dish was in a manila envelope that had strings around it, and on the strings was red wax stamped with the distinctive seals of Luigi Gonella and Giovanni Riggi. As Riggi was cutting the seal, I snapped pictures with my camera, knowing that it was important to document the authenticity of the samples I would be studying. Riggi finished opening the case and took out the three segments of linen for our research. The pieces—A, B, and C—were from the area exactly in contact with the parts of fabric that had been radiocarbon dated. There was no doubt that it was the same material. At the time of the radiocarbon dating Testore and Riggi thought that the edge might be contaminated, which is why they had cut off the trimmings. The weight of each of these trimmings was reported by Dr. Testore in Paris in September 1989, during the symposium organized by CIELT, a French group. We took more than two hundred photographs of the samples through the microscope. When I saw the three segments from the Shroud, I realized the huge responsibility that I was undertaking and was extremely worried. I had a flashback to my college exams, shaking inside while observing the samples. I knew that the next few minutes could mean the invalidation of the radiocarbon dating done in 1988 if I found an unsuspected contaminant like the bioplastic coating. All the equipment we had brought from San Antonio was in Riggi's library.

In addition to the three pieces of textile, Riggi had pieces of Scotch tape with blood samples taken from the back of the head, the occipital area. Some of these tapes held what looked like blood globules. There were fibers with blood on them, and others were simply "image" fibers, with no apparent bloodstains. He also had some boxes with dust that had been vacuumed from the Shroud. Even though they had used sophisticated forensic laboratory equipment to pick up the dust, I did not want to spend too much time on it because of the likelihood of contamination. Such contamination could easily have come at any moment over the past centuries. But we began our examination by looking at the dust with the optical microscope, though I did not think it would be of much help. I knew the critical moment would be when I could examine a linen thread under the microscope to check for the presence of the bioplastic coating. So when Riggi removed a thread from the trimmed edge, I was nervous as I put it under the microscope. My nervousness did not last long; immediately, I saw a bioplastic coating on the fibers. I quickly took a picture with the microscope camera and called to Father Cervantes and to Riggi, "It's there! There's bioplastic coating on the sample!" Even an untrained viewer could see the fibers of the thread completely covered with bioplastic coating, as well as some fungi, clear interference in the radiocarbon dating. Each of us took turns looking at the fibers, and it struck us all that somehow this coating was a thing of beauty in itself. It was an incredible moment for all of us.

When we looked at the fibers on the Scotch tape from the occipital area, we saw that they were not uniform in size. Later, we established that they varied between 10 microns and 30 microns, depending on the weight of each fiber and the amount of bioplastic deposit. An occasional image fiber had coating even thicker than the fiber itself. It took just a few seconds to recognize that these fibers must be image fibers. Under the microscope the areas that appear solid when the light is behind them are a pale mauve to carmine in color. When we looked at them in high magnification we saw that they contained particulate matter. Because I knew what ancient blood looked like under the microscope, I identified it as blood. Father Cervantes was crying, crying like a baby from happiness. Riggi, looking at the fibers, had a different but equally happy reaction: he brought out an old brandy for us to toast the discovery! Riggi was convinced from the moment he saw the coating. With our spirits high, we spent the rest of the evening celebrating and wondering about the implications of this finding.

The next stage was to ask Riggi whether I could take some samples back to San Antonio for further study. When I requested a few threads, he said that that was what the samples were for. It was indeed a generous act on Riggi's part, since, as guardian of the samples, he put his responsibility on the line in trusting me. And he was to receive nothing in return. All I had to offer was my dedication to honest and thorough study of the samples. Riggi kept the bulk of the three pieces of textile, but as he cut some threads for me, they sounded brittle, and it struck me as an indication of the presence of something more than mere fabric. When, with fine scissors, I cut a thread myself, it was as if I were cutting a plasticized fishing line or a series of thin copper wires, very different from the feeling I got when cutting a thread from a contemporary piece of linen. Riggi also gave me one of the Scotch tape pieces he had taken from the occipital area on the Shroud in 1988. I carried the samples back on microscope slides, protected with cover slips, in a small plastic box. I was in ecstasy! Can you imagine! Having the opportunity to study samples of the Shroud . . .

Chapter 4

"ARRIVEDERCI
ROMA"

R IDING WAVE AFTER WAVE OF DISCOVERY, EACH MO-
ment more powerful than the last, was a heady experience
for me. Though the findings encouraged me to continue working
hard, the excitement led me to make decisions that may not have been
the best. Perhaps I should not have returned to Italy, on June 9, 1993,
to attend the scientific symposium organized in Rome by the French
group CIELT, the Center for International Studies on the Shroud of
Turin. I took counsel from Father Cervantes, who had told me about
the symposium, and I was so buoyed up by the attention my hypothesis was gaining that I decided to share my ideas with the delegates by
reading my paper "Biogenic Varnish and the Shroud of Turin."

By the time I reached the decision, the conference was only a
month away, so I had several phone conversations with the CIELT
organizers to make a case for my delivering the paper. It became
obvious during the course of our phone calls that they were less than
enthusiastic about accepting a paper so late in the day, and they also
seemed not wholly enthusiastic about the subject of my talk. The

situation was not helped by the existence of a language barrier, since I do not speak French and had to communicate through an interpreter. Instead of referring to an adequate French scientific reference book, they took my mention of molds to mean mushrooms, and kept repeating *"champignons"* when I tried to explain my theory about bacteria and microcolonial black fungi. They did, however, eventually respond positively, and I soon received a letter requesting an abstract of my paper and allotting me fifteen minutes in which to present it.

Once again my traveling companion was the spirited Father Cervantes. We flew to Rome and then drove to the outskirts of the city. The symposium was being held at the Domus Mariae, a former convent. Needless to say, the accommodations at a convent are not what one would have at a world-class hotel, so I was not expecting great things. Even so, I was a little surprised to find that my room was four by eight feet, and the temperature in the room was about 100 degrees! The conference hall was also stifling. But the worst part was that breakfast was a piece of bread and a cup of coffee. This must be why nuns are supposed to go to heaven!

As I listened to papers and talked to the other attendees, I was disappointed to find that there were not many scientists. Most of those I met were unaware of basic research methods and were poorly informed about current Shroud research. I began to feel that this might not be the best audience to whom to unveil my new hypothesis and findings.

True to my fears, the meeting did not go well. As I gave my presentation, I could sense that most people were not following what I said. And they were very skeptical, particularly when I said that the image was caused by the relative thickness of the bioplastic coating. As soon as I said that, I seemed to lose my audience completely. Afterward, I went around to talk to people individually, asking if they believed that the deposit of bacteria could produce an image. Except for one person, everyone said it was impossible. The only person who thought it possible was Father Fred Brinkmann, President of the Holy Shroud Guild here in America. Most felt that some undefinable miracle had caused the image, and that describing the image as the result of bacteria did not seem fitting. But to me, a wondrous event is no less a miracle because we know the mechanics of its coming to be. In the case of the image on the Shroud, I feel perfectly comfortable saying that bacteria could have been the agent of this miracle.

Some of the CIELT officials said that if I thought the *champignons* were the reason for the inaccuracy of the radiocarbon dating, then the Shroud should be radiocarbon dated again. I explained that it was not so simple. Even if the process was repeated, using the same preparation of the samples, the age would be even younger than was declared in 1988, because the bacteria are still alive and still producing a deposit. I didn't feel I was making much progress, so I closed my mouth. I had accomplished what I had gone to Rome to do, to give my report. At least it was available for posterity.

But although the business side of the trip was a disappointment, the social side was not. I had excellent food and shared the joy experienced by my traveling companion, Father Cervantes, whose trip to Rome was the first since he had studied there as a seminarian back in the 1940s. After my report we went to the Sistine Chapel and then did more sightseeing in Rome. Though Father Cervantes was in his seventies, he had more energy than I. After we had walked for about four hours, he would say, "Pinch me so that I know that I am not dreaming." In the evening we would each enjoy a Scotch on the rocks in the bar of the Domus Mariae before retiring to bed.

I will never forget our last day in Rome. While we were dining at a restaurant in the Plazza Navona, we were serenaded by an accordion player accompanied by a mandolin player. They played "Arrivederci Roma." At that moment, tears came to Father Cervantes's eyes.

I owe all my Shroud research to Father Cervantes. Had he not talked to Gonella and Riggi, I would not have been able to do my research. He translated into Italian the protocol we presented to Riggi, and it is now in his archives. That is why I dedicate this book to him. He died on January 20, 1995.

Chapter 5

THE BACTERIA
ARE ALIVE!

N OT DISCOURAGED BY MY RECEPTION IN ROME, I RE-
turned to San Antonio determined to continue my microbiological studies on the Shroud samples given to me by Riggi the previous month. I sent portions of the samples to the University of Washington in Seattle to be studied with the electron microscope (SEM and
backscattered electron microscope) and took a small thread piece to
the Chemistry Department of the Southwest Research Institute, which
has a group of infra-red absorption microscopists (FT-IR). Almost all
of my studies were done in my laboratory at home and in the
Microbiology Department of the Santa Rosa Hospital in San Antonio, with whose staff I have had a happy working relationship for
more than eight years. Adolphus Smith, a microbiology technician,
and Vicky Fitzhugh, the director of the microbiology laboratory, have
been especially helpful to me. I have also had assistance from Brian
Tindall, at DSMZ Braunschweig, Germany, and Karl Schleifer of
Technische Universitat, Munich.

At home, I used an optical microscope to study the samples from
Riggi. Even with low magnifications, I could see that the thread had a

surprising luster. This was something that Ian Wilson had described on his examination of the Shroud in 1973: "The linen, although ivory-coloured with age, was still surprisingly clean looking, even to the extent of a damask-like surface sheen." At a magnification of X80 I could see the reason for this: the fibers had a yellowish bioplastic coating, with millions of bacteria and dark brown fungi. Using a higher magnification, I saw the bacteria and fungi, showing up as a fishnet of filaments. With a scanning electron microscope, I found that the fibers were completely covered by the bioplastic coating (polyhydroxyalkanoate) and by many colonies of fungi, which usually thrive on this polymer. Some fibers had at their crests a pink pigment produced by the bacteria.

Examining the fibers from the Scotch tape from the back of the head, I could see that some looked as if they had a blood deposit and a thick coating of a golden-yellow material, with many of the blue-green bacteria and also many dark brown fungi. Some fibers from the same area were image fibers but did not appear to have any blood and were yellow in color, and the coating appeared thicker than the non-image fibers. Fibers from the threads taken from the edge of the samples, where there was no image, were pale yellow, and the coating was thinner than in the other areas. Fungi were also visible on these latter areas. Under ultraviolet light, the fibers had a strong yellowish-green fluorescence.

Using a polarizing microscope and cross polars on fibers from image and non-image portions, I was able to see highly organized mineral crystals of calcite, quartz, iron oxide, and manganese oxide. They were deposited on both types of fibers, but were more numerous on the image fibers. Testing done at the University of Washington facility by Dr. Paul Bierman showed that their sample had a composition similar to that of the desert varnish on ancient artifacts. Some areas of the bioplastic coating were high in manganese, some had a high iron content, and some a high calcium content. An electron microscope with backscattered light confirmed the presence of these mineral deposits, which led me to conclude that the coating produced by the bacteria had both mineral and organic elements. The presence of iron was of particular interest, because it confirmed what Walter McCrone had found when he examined fibers on tapes from the 1978 testing of the Shroud, although my explanation of its presence is very different from his, as we shall see later.

Some of the fibers were mounted on a slide and put under the infra-red microscope for spectroscopy. As with the optical microscope, the organic component of the bioplastic coating was immediately obvious. But what was especially interesting was the comparison of the "spectrum" or graph obtained from the Shroud with the graph obtained from one of my Maya artifacts and from a clay bowl from Apatzingan, Michoacán, Mexico. The three were similar, but when they were compared with a spectrum from a sample of pure cellulose, used as a control, they were different. Again, this was to prove an important finding, for if the samples dated by the radiocarbon laboratories had been pure cellulose, as was claimed, then the spectra should have been similar. That they were not, immediately suggested that the cellulose in the samples dated in 1988 had an extra organic component, namely, the bioplastic coating.

A fascinating aspect of the research was that, using twelve different culture media, we were able to grow bacteria and fungi from samples taken from the textile of the Shroud of Turin. So far we have isolated three types of bacteria and four types of fungi. A particularly important species is a pink-pigment-producing and PHA-producing bacterium that I have named *Leobacillus rubrus* (genus nov. species nov.). As of now, it is unique to the Shroud and can live under a variety of different conditions. The Leobacillus grows faster when given a 10 percent boost in carbon dioxide.

The increase in the production of the pink pigment by the Leobacillus when there is an increase in carbon dioxide explains the phenomenon described in 1931 by Don Antonio Tonelli. When he saw the Shroud exhibited on May 3 of that year, he described the bloodlike stains as having an orange-red color, but when he saw the Shroud again three weeks later, he noticed that the color of the bloodstains had changed to violet-red. We now know, some sixty-seven years later, that the color change was caused by the rapid growth of the bacteria in the increased carbon dioxide being breathed out by the faithful who flocked to look at the Shroud. We also know from our culture experiments that under normal conditions, as would have been obtained when the Shroud was rolled up in its casket, the bacteria grow very slowly, and it takes them a long time to produce the pigment. But the fact that we were able to grow bacteria at all was an exciting finding, with implications for the dating done by the radiocarbon laboratories. If no cultures had grown, that would have indicated that the surface of the Shroud was completely inert. But bacteria and fungi from the Shroud thrived in certain laboratory conditions. For example, when a segment of a Shroud thread was grown in a Sabouraud dextrose agar plate and examined four months later, the bioplastic coating was seen to have increased markedly, thanks to the activity of the bacteria. This showed that they were still alive, growing, and accruing modern radiocarbon. So what the radiocarbon laboratories had tested was a mixture of carbon from the original linen, and new carbon from the bioplastic coating produced by the bacteria! It was this that caused the Shroud to be dated as medieval. And this was the reason for my telling the CIELT officials that if the carbon dating was repeated under the very same conditions as before, the new date would be even younger, because the bacteria would have multiplied with the passage of time, skewing the dating even further.

I made one finding, shortly after my return from Turin, that initially was an interesting diversion from the main area of research on the microbiology of the Shroud. When the fibers from the "blood" area of the back of the head were stained with Wright's stain at the Histology Department of Santa Rosa Hospital, a structure was found that looked as if it had been woven. At first, I thought it might be from a headband, made of very thin threads of camel hair. But nearly two years later, by chance I saw a similar structure in a mycology book, and I realized that my initial hunch was entirely wrong. The structure is not manmade; it is a Cleistothecium, a structure of the fungus of the genus *Aspergillus,* formed during its sexual stage. This fungus grows on ancient wood.

Excited by my findings, I wrote them up as "Bioplastic Coating on the Shroud of Turin, A Preliminary Report," December 1993. Through Father Fred Brinkmann, I obtained the correct address of His Holiness Pope John Paul II, and, by Federal Express, sent copies of this report to both His Holiness and to Father Brinkmann. Father Fred received his on December 24, an early Christmas present, and obviously the Pope received his copy, for the following year I received a letter from Monsignor L. Sandri, dated April 12, 1994:

> *His Holiness Pope John Paul II has received your letter and enclosure, and he has asked me to send you this acknowledgment. He appreciates the sentiments which prompted you to send him your research on the Holy Shroud.*
>
> *His Holiness will remember you in his prayers, and he invokes upon you God's abundant blessings.*

Little did I know that five years later, on July 29, 1998, I would be able to give to His Holiness, in person and directly into his hand at Vatican City, my last report of the Shroud of Turin, *The DNA of God?*

I also sent three copies of the report to Riggi, one for him, one for Luigi Gonella, and one for Cardinal Saldarini. I did not learn until later that Riggi had never passed on to the Cardinal the copy intended for him.

Chapter 6

DNA

IN THE BLOOD . . .

T HE QUESTION AS TO WHETHER THE SHROUD BEARS deposits of blood produces an answer that reflects the person answering the question. In Italy, Dr. Baima Bollone, who had taken samples from the "blood" areas with sticky tape, reported that yes, there was blood, and it was of the AB group. In the opposite side, Dr. Walter McCrone, also using sticky tape, reported that the marks are not blood, but are the pigments red ochre and vermillion, as used by an artist. Dr. Adler and Dr. Heller, having examined the tapes used by Dr. McCrone, came to the conclusion that the stains were indeed blood. Faced with these differences of opinion, I decided that the area was worthy of further investigation.

My first examination of the sample sent to me by Dr. Adler, taken from the left-hand area, where there should have been blood, was not encouraging. Even if blood was there when the sample was taken in 1978, it had been completely replaced by bacteria and fungi. All I could tell with the optical microscope was that the material was organic, not crystalline pigments, as reported by McCrone.

The blood sample from the back of the head, which I had

brought back from Turin, courtesy of Giovanni Riggi, was my first breakthrough. When I looked at the sample under the optical microscope, I found only a small area that showed blood. The rest was filled with bacteria and fungi. Under the guidance of Dr. Victor Saldivar, a pathologist at the Santa Rosa Hospital, I saw the samples being stained. Wright's stain, commonly used for the procedure, showed that the smear had been almost completely replaced by fungi. When the iron of the remaining portion was stained with Mallory's Prussian blue, it was found that, of the total bloodstain area, only 5 percent still showed blood; the remaining 95 percent had been replaced by bacteria and fungi. The tests proved, however, that there was human blood on the samples, even if only in very small amounts. The immunohisto-chemical tests we conducted showed that the blood on the Shroud was of the AB group. In the general world population the AB blood group is rare (3.2 percent), but it is 600 percent more common (18 percent) in the "Babylonian" Jews, and the Jews from northern Palestine, the cultural groups with highest incidence of AB blood group. The finding of the AB blood group suggests two different cell lines of the man on the Shroud, but it is not as dramatic as the finding of the two sexual chromosomes X and Y that I will report later. The AB blood group in western Europeans and in Americans is not that common. (We did not have enough blood sample to test for the rhesus factor.) It was interesting that our findings supported the claims of Baima Bollone back in Italy. Both Dr. Saldivar and the technician in charge of running the tests in the Histology Department knew that they were dealing with samples from the Shroud, and Dr. Saldivar joked, "I am happy that the Bishop is not here. If he was here, he would have us kneeling, looking at the slides."

Having seen for myself how little actual blood remained on my samples, I began to doubt some of Dr. Adler's comments. For example, he said that the color of the blood on the Shroud, which is surprisingly red, rather than the brown one might expect in ancient blood, was caused by the presence of high proportions of bilirubin, a bile pigment that increases with severe trauma, such as might have been caused by injuries inflicted before the crucifixion. I doubt this is the case, for he referred to the color of the entire bloodstain, and the area that still has blood is too small to discern with the naked eye. The carmine color of the image, I believe, was caused by the pigment from the surface bacteria. The stains certainly look as if they came from the original wounds, but the blood in the stains has been replaced by the bacteria and fungi, especially the fungi, which used the blood for food and energy to promote their growth.

Now, thoroughly immersed in the microbiology of both the Shroud of Turin and other ancient artifacts, I wanted to explore different avenues, to take the research further. A member of the Department of Microbiology at the university suggested that I talk to Professor Stephen Mattingly, a microbiologist at the University of Texas Health Science Center in San Antonio. At his invitation, I went to his department, where we discussed future lines of research. I was especially interested in isolating bacteria from ancient artifacts, both the Shroud and the Maya examples. Mattingly felt that this microbiology topic might be eligible for a National Science Foundation grant. After reading my curriculum vitae, he invited me to join his department as Adjunct Professor of Microbiology, which I did in September of 1994. I spent a year expanding my research, funded partly by the grant that came through for the department.

This led to a fruitful research program in microbiology and DNA studies conducted on the white blood cell remnants present in the blood globules from the occipital region. I explained my problems with the blood to Dr. Victor Tryon, Director of the Center for Advanced DNA Technology at UTHSC at San Antonio, where a technique known as polymerase chain reaction (PCR) is regularly used for establishing the DNA make-up of samples. Dr. Tryon knew that the sample we were using came from the Shroud of Turin. One cannot hide the purpose of research when depending on the advice of an expert in the field. But Nancy Mitchell Tryon, Dr. Tryon's wife, who actually ran the samples through the PCR equipment, was not aware of the origin of the sample.

The human genome has more than 100,000 genes, formed by three billion base pairs. Tryon advised that we try cloning the easiest of the genes that could be obtained from ancient blood, the beta-globin gene. What we were not sure of was whether the blood, which we knew from the work at the Santa Rosa Hospital was present, would be too degraded for cloning. Fortunately, our fears were unfounded, and Nancy M. Tryon was able to clone the blood sample and amplify it. A blood globule from the five tiny collections on the Scotch tape was used, and the betaglobin gene segment from chromosome 11 was cloned. This proved conclusively that there was ancient blood on the Shroud. We could not, of course, tell from whom it had come, nor whether that person had Semitic blood. (For this type of investigation you need to clone the short DNA segments generally known as minisatellites.) Nor could we ascertain how old the blood was. Obviously there was the possibility of contamination and the possibility that blood from someone other than the crucified victim happened to fall on the part of the Shroud from which the sample was taken. But it is certainly more likely that the blood came from the Man on the Shroud, rather than a bystander, in view of the fact that the sample was taken from the back of the head, from the area where the crown of thorns would have damaged the head of the victim.

G. Riggi was happy with the news I imparted by telephone, as was everyone in Dr. Tryon's laboratory. But at this stage, all we could say about the blood was that it was ancient, because of the degree of degradation of the small amount of blood we found on our sample, and that it had come from a human being or high primate. Nothing more. The next stage of the research was to uncover evidence that could have been regarded as controversial, and that was to be followed by another stage with even more potential for sensationalism.

In order to proceed with the research, we needed more samples, and this involved another approach to Riggi. I had already decided to invite him to the second of a series of round tables I was organizing for June 1994, and he, eager to see what further information we might glean, agreed to bring more samples with him. On his arrival, on June 4, he handed Dr. Tryon samples from the occipital area that he had taken in 1988. Because the testing takes several days, Riggi returned to Italy to await the outcome.

In order to establish the sex of the individual, one can look for the testis-determining factor (TDF), which is positive only in the male. If you don't find it, however, you cannot conclude that your sample is from a female; it may be that something went wrong during the testing procedure. Another way to determine the sex is to clone the genes amelogenin-X and amelogenin-Y, and that is what Dr. Tryon advised. Again he was right; the PCR technique enabled us to isolate the amelogenin-X gene from chromosome X and the amelogenin-Y gene from chromosome Y. I telephoned Riggi that same day. It was already eleven at night in Italy, but, half asleep, he understood, from my mixture of Spanish and English, that we had proved that the blood on the Shroud had belonged to a human male.

But this finding in itself was to prove intriguing. Did we have evidence to disprove the Mystery of the Virgin birth? In the case of the Man on the Shroud, did the presence of the Y gene indicate that he had been conceived as a result of normal sexual intercourse? Our analysis showed the blood to have come from a male. I could not prove that the blood had come from Jesus of Nazareth, but until I find a scientific reason to show that this was not from Jesus Christ, I will maintain my belief that it belonged to Jesus of Nazareth.

So if we believed that this sample came from Jesus, who, the Gospels tell us, was conceived of a Virgin, where did the Y chromosome come from? Did we have proof that the Virgin birth was a great myth? I believe in the Mystery of the Incarnate Word, but even medicine is able to explain conception in virgin girls in some rare cases of tumors in the ovary. Some of these tumors of the ovary have formation of embryos, known as *parthenogenetic pregnancies*.

In 1956, J. H. Tjio and A. Levan reported that the number of nuclear chromosomes in the human species is 46 (44 autosomes or nonsex chromosomes in addition to two sexual chromosomes). The normal male has 44 autosomes plus XY, the normal female has 44 autosomes plus XX. A male sperm contains half the number of chromosomes—that is, either 22 plus the X chromosome or 22 plus the Y chromosome—and the female ovum contains 22 plus X. At conception, the resulting embryo receives the full complement of autosomes plus a pair of sex chromosomes. The sex of the new individual depends on which of the sex chromosomes is supplied by the male. If it is the X chromosome, it combines with the X chromosome from the mother and produces a female (XX). If it is the Y chromosome, it combines with the X chromosome from the mother and produces a male (XY).

I have been a pediatrician for thirty years. For reasons of patient confidentiality, I cannot give dates or names in the following case history, but I want to describe it to show that our findings about the chromosomal make-up of the Man on the Shroud were not evidence of sexual activity on the part of the Virgin Mary, as might have been indicated at first sight.

This case concerns a thirteen-year-old girl, brought to my office by her father, with whom she was living after the separation of the parents. The girl had nausea and vomiting in the morning and was complaining of severe abdominal pain. She had some vaginal bleeding. There was also a large mass in the lower abdomen, about 25 to 30 centimeters in diameter. The girl claimed to be a virgin, but I have had many cases of twelve- and thirteen-year-old pregnant girls who denied having had sexual intercourse, but whose pregnancies were normally produced. The two pregnancy tests done on this patient were both positive. If the mass had been centrally located in the abdomen, I would have assumed that the girl was pregnant, as the tests indicated. But the mass was to the right of the abdomen, so I considered an ovarian cyst or an ovarian tumor. It was necessary to investigate gynecologically if the girl was a virgin, and this proved to be the case. She was admitted to hospital and operated on for the removal of a tumor, which had probably been growing in her for two or three months.

Thin sections of the tumor prepared at the histology laboratory showed that the tumor was a *polyembryoma*. This is a tumor that grows in the ovary and produces embryoids. Since the tumor was produced without sexual intercourse, it is parthenogenetic. In the case I studied, there were several embryoids with XX chromosomes. When an ovarian mixed-germ-cell tumor contains cells from a *polyembryoma* and cells from a *gonadoblastoma,* the embryoids may have XY chromosomes; that is, male embryoids in a virgin patient. There were only eight cases of *polyembryomas* reported in the medical literature before mine. I had been looking for a case like this for ten years, so I felt fortunate in seeing this one. I want to stress again that this case is different from the mystery of the Immaculate Conception, but it shows that the finding of blood with X and Y chromosomes does not prove that the Man on the Shroud was not Jesus of Nazareth. If each year on January 1 we celebrate the Feast of the Circumcision of the Lord, the genetic formula of Jesus of Nazareth has to be 46 chromosomes (44 autosomes and XY).

But our doing research into the DNA of the Man on the Shroud has now become controversial. Since the recent cloning of a sheep, Dolly, the idea of cloning from DNA has been greeted with horror by many people who view it as interfering with the usual biological methods of reproduction. "Sensationalist" reporting of the DNA work that we conducted on the Shroud has added to the unease many "Shroudies" felt when they heard about my research. Indeed, that may well explain the evident distress in a letter I received from Cardinal Saldarini on July 31, 1996, accusing me of having no respect for the religious beliefs of millions.

I have no problem with the research I conducted. The DNA mol-

ecule is made up of a twisted helix, like two strands of yarn. One is
the coding DNA strand, and the other is a template of that strand.
The strands are joined by base pairs of chemicals in a sort of code,
and life is transferred from one organism to another by DNA, en-
closed in the nucleus of cells in long threads known as chromosomes.
Usually the DNA of ancient blood is partly destroyed. That means
that segments of the molecule no longer exist, and we have only
pieces of it. In order to clone a person, we need most of that person's
DNA. In the case of the Shroud, the amount of blood we have is very
little; because 95 percent of it has, over time, been replaced by bacteria and fungi. The blood that is left is so degraded that the few short
segments still present are not sufficient to allow the cloning of a person. In our research we have cloned only three short segments of three
genes. From the betaglobin gene from chromosome 11 we have a
segment of only 268 base pairs. From the amelogenin-X gene, which
produces the enamel on teeth, we have only about 250 base pairs, and
the same number from amelogenin-Y. The difference between amelogenin-X and amelogenin-Y is in the size of the two genes, but we
have only short segments of each.

As I mentioned earlier, the number of base pairs making up a
human genome or complete pattern is three billion. We have only
between 700 and 750 base pairs, so we are far short of having a
complete genome. Nor do I think that we would ever be able to have
the complete genome of the Man on the Shroud. And I believe this is
for the best. That is why I say that I have no problem with the research I have conducted.

Do I think that we have the DNA of God? If we review the first
Four Ecumenical Councils that clarified the divinity of Jesus of Nazareth (Nicea in 325, Constantinople in 361, Ephesus in 431, and Chalcedon in 451), we may find the answer. In the Council of Nicea, or
First Ecumenical Council, the Emperor Constantine and three hundred bishops were present. It was declared that Jesus of Nazareth was
"true God from true God." In the Council of Constantinople, or

Second Ecumenical Council, it was declared that *"the Father, the Son, and the Holy Spirit are uncreated and are to be worshiped together as one God."* In the Council of Ephesus, or Third Ecumenical Council, it was established that *"Virgin Mary was the Mother of God or 'Theotokos.'"* Finally, in the Council of Chalcedon or Fourth Ecumenical Council, it was declared that Jesus Christ was *"truly God and truly man."* So if the blood from the Man on the Shroud is the blood of Jesus of Nazareth, my answer to the question of whether or not we have the DNA of God is *Yes.*

Chapter 7

THE REDATING
THAT WENT WRONG

I T WAS NOW TIME TO TAKE STOCK OF MY RESEARCH FIND-
ings and draw up a plan for possible future research. Thanks to
the "experts" in New York who challenged the authenticity of my
Maya artifacts, I studied the secondary weathering on them so that I
could prove they were genuine. What I found was the bioplastic coating, which I was able to scrape off easily and study with the SEM and
radiocarbon dating. But although the carbon dating showed that the
artifact was old, it gave an age for the Itzamna Tun that proved too
"young" for the time when it probably was created. This discrepancy
between the radiocarbon age and the true age, I have explained, must
have been caused by the bioplastic coating. And if that was true of
these objects, I believed it would also be true of other ancient artifacts, especially of the Turin Shroud, whose carbon date was already a
subject of debate.

This pointed to our next task: to study and, if possible, isolate
the bioplastic coating so that we could prepare an entirely "pure"
sample of the Shroud, devoid of any contaminants, for more precise
radiocarbon dating. To do this research, we needed more samples,

because the ones Riggi had supplied were not suitable for radiocarbon dating. For that, we needed a sample of the textile rather than the threads or Scotch tape samples.

I am in debt to Giovanni Riggi, and always will be, and also to Luigi Gonella. When I explained to Riggi what I hoped to do, and why I needed to clear a sample of any of the contaminating plastic coating so that I could have a new radiocarbon dating done, Riggi was hesitant. He was reluctant to release samples that, of necessity, would be destroyed in the testing. Quite correctly, he asked me for a written protocol of what I proposed to do, and I got it to him in September 1994. Because of some health problems, Riggi was unable to travel at this time, but to my delight, he read the protocol and agreed to bring samples to San Antonio for the project: "The Digestion, Analysis, and Radiocarbon Dating of the Bioplastic Coating and Linen Fragments of the Shroud of Turin." I met Riggi at the airport on November 5, took him to his hotel, and, next day, escorted him to the university, where we began to prepare the textile for the production of what we hoped would be a pure glucose sample to be tested by the AMS laboratories in Arizona and Toronto. We weighed the samples with the excellent scales I usually reserve for my gemology studies, and then began the cleaning operation.

In order to prove the presence of the bioplastic coating, we followed the identical cleaning process used by the laboratories that conducted the radiocarbon dating back in 1988. The original laboratories, in Oxford, Zürich, and Arizona, had split their samples into smaller samples, and, using different concentrations of chemicals, had followed basically the same cleaning procedure, an "acid-base-acid" washing. They used hydrochloric acid, sometimes at slightly different dilutions, followed by sodium hydroxide, followed by a further washing with hydrochloric acid. The samples were washed with distilled water between each stage of treatment.

We followed exactly the same procedure, after which I used the optical microscope to examine some of the fibers that were supposedly "clean." Nothing had changed. The fibers stayed the same; the bioplastic coating was still visible. That meant the original laboratories unintentionally had not done a good cleaning job. Their method cleaned the samples of *some* of the contaminants, but not of the bioplastic coating or the bacteria. They intended to remove calcium carbonates, wax, and some of the organic material that was present. But the bacteria were not cleaned off. The bacteria on the Shroud grow in alkaline environments and were very happy that they were still being fed the sodium hydroxide solution.

We decided to separate the bioplastic coating. With a higher concentration of sodium hydroxide, we could destroy the flax but not the coating. While trying, with forceps, to remove some flax fibers from the threads, I caused part of the plastic to break, leaving the naked flax fibers. The higher sodium hydroxide solutions destroyed the flax, leaving the empty bioplastic tubes; it was as if a plastic ballpoint pen had had the ink tube removed. I took several photographs of these empty plastic tubes, which are responsible for the Shroud's sheen, visible to the naked eye. What was especially important was that the plastic tube we retained was more than 60 percent of the overall amount of fiber. Professor Hall, when countering attacks on the dating of the Shroud, stated that a contamination of more than 60 percent would be needed to skew the radiocarbon dating results. He did not believe that was possible. Well, here was the proof . . .

I have grown bacteria cultures from the Shroud even after the acid-base-acid cleaning, which means that the bacteria present in the empty tubes continued to grow. Again, the living bacteria were responsible for distorting the radiocarbon dating results, and, because they are alive, will continue to distort any future dating, making the cloth appear even younger.

We now know that the 1988 samples used in the dating of the Shroud had cellulose from the flax and also bacteria, a small number of fungi, and the bioplastic coating. Our task was to prepare a sample for testing without these contaminants. We used four small pieces

from two of the three trimming segments that Riggi had brought on
his second visit.

Our next objective was to produce pure glucose from the cellulose of the flax fibers. The enzyme cellulase would have destroyed
only the flax, not the plastic coating. That is, we would have been left
with glucose instead of cellulose. The cellulose is like a rosary of
glucose molecules. The enzymes from the cellulase group (endoglu-
canase, exoglucanase, and beta-glucosidase) cut the unions of the cellulose molecules, so we would have ended up with pure glucose.

The segments of textile were crushed in a sterile mortar with a
pestle and glass beads. The resulting powder was placed in a sterile
test tube. Commercially prepared cellulase enzyme obtained from *Aspergillus niger* fungi was mixed with Tris-borate as a buffer so that
the cellulase group of enzymes could digest the cellulose. The mixture
was kept at 37° centigrade for twenty-four hours. After that, as expected, it proved positive for glucose. The liquid was filtered through
a 500-dalton filter, which allows molecules of a molecular weight less
than 500 to pass through. Only the glucose (molecular weight 180)
and cellobiose (two molecules of glucose beta-bonded with a weight
of 360) would be able to pass through. The cellulase could not, because of its high molecular weight, nor could the plastic coating,
which was not affected by the cellulase. We collected the liquid, dried
it in a lyophilization machine, and obtained a powder. We prepared
the sample to take it to Arizona for radiocarbon testing. A job well
done—or so we thought.

Riggi and I flew to the AMS laboratory in Arizona and handed
the sample personally to Dr. Timothy Jull, who was going to run the
radiocarbon dating from the powder. Jull took half of the sample,
and my wife, Maria, and I flew to New York with the remaining half
to give to Dr. Harry Gove. He then took it to the Accelerator Mass
Spectrometry Facility at the University of Toronto and told them of
the sample's origin. Because the Arizona laboratory had been involved in the original testing of the Shroud, we did not tell Jull that he

was dealing with a sample from the Shroud. We told him that it was from an ancient Egyptian textile. He did not suspect Riggi, because there are several ancient Egyptian mummies in Turin, and Riggi had samples from some of them.

The results came back in December 1994. Arizona had dated the sample back approximately 5000 years—3000 years before Jesus of Nazareth. Toronto had dated it 800 years younger, but still too old for the Shroud. Even allowing for statistical error, these dates were too far apart, given that it was exactly the same sample being tested by the two laboratories. Between them, the laboratories had cast doubt on the accuracy of the test. Once again, the carbon dating technique had been found wanting.

We had prepared what we thought were pure samples, and we expected them to show a date of around A.D. 30, assuming that the Shroud was from the time of the crucifixion of Jesus of Nazareth. But when I looked at the results, I knew something was very wrong.

In science, one can never, never, ever falsify any findings; sooner or later it will backfire. That is why I feel it necessary to explain the mistake we made in the radiocarbon dating of our sample. We had contamination from a death carbon (an oil derivative with no carbon 14 because it is millions of years old). The buffer we used for the cellulase activity contained a petroleum-based chemical that caused our results to be wrong. We needed a buffer for the enzymatic action, and I mistakenly asked Mattingly whether that buffer, Tris-borate, was like boric acid, an inorganic material (that is, one that does not contain carbon), instead of looking into it myself. He said it was just a borate. But after the radiocarbon dating and the evidence that something had gone wrong, I studied the whole mechanism. With the aid of a book on chemical compounds, I discovered that the Tris-borate indeed had some organic material—it contained carbon!

A brief recapitulation of the mechanics of carbon dating may be of help in understanding why this mistake was so unfortunate. All living things take in carbon dioxide, including a tiny proportion of the radioactive isotope carbon 14, which is formed in the upper atmosphere by the bombardment of the cosmic rays on nitrogen atoms; these are transformed into carbon 14. The carbon 14 becomes an integral part of plants and bacteria that use carbon dioxide and, from them, part of other living organisms. After the death of the organism, the carbon 14 in it begins to decay, becoming nitrogen again. The halfway stage, or half-life, is about 5730 years, so if, after the organism's death, we measure the remaining carbon 14 and carbon 12, we should, theoretically, be able to ascertain the date of death. In the case of the Shroud, we should have been able to work out the date of the flax, which was probably harvested around about the time of the crucifixion. But by adding carbon from the Tris-borate buffer, we inadvertently altered the proportional relationship of the carbon 12 to carbon 14, thus ruining what should have been a definitive piece of research. We needed a "buffer" to ensure that the enzymatic reaction of the cellulase continued to work. Without it, the pH, or level of acidity/alkalinity, of our test mixture would have changed, stopping the breakdown of cellulose into pure glucose. Had we used another type of buffer, such as one with a phosphate base, we would almost certainly have had a perfect test result.

Reactions to this mistake were predictable. Mattingly was upset because his advice about the buffer was not correct. Riggi was upset because most of his trimmings sample had been destroyed, with no satisfactory outcome. Jull looked at what appeared to be reasonable results, but I then told him he had been dealing with the Shroud, and the war of Troy started again! Jull said this was not the correct way of doing things. I explained that we did not want anyone to know we were doing a blind test, but he said that was the wrong way to do a blind test. I received a very critical letter from Warren Beck of the AMS Facility in Arizona a few days later.

If we set aside the mistake, what are the implications of our research for the original radiocarbon-dating laboratories? In 1988 the carbon dating scientists were so confident about their technique that they misjudged their cleaning methods. Radiocarbon dating is an excellent technique and will give a correct dating for a sample, but it will not send up a warning signal if that sample is contaminated. If you have pure glucose after the digestion of the cellulose by cellulases, you will have a pure sample and will get a correct date. The problem with the radiocarbon scientists, was that they were overconfident; they were sure they had the final answer. But I believe that in this life, sooner or later, each of us receives a lesson in humility, and this is their lesson. Mine was in not checking the chemical composition of the Tris-borate. You can never say in science that there is nothing new that will appear or that you are 100 percent correct. You need to leave room for new possibilities, for new findings, for new vistas. None of the great scientists I have known has been absolutely sure. I believe that the big numbers written on the blackboard on October 13, 1988—"1260–1390!"—with the revealing exclamation mark, was a sign of arrogance. Even if that was the true radiocarbon date of the sample, as I believe it was, that does not mean it was the radiocarbon date of the Shroud. The sample had contaminants. The scientists had an answer to the amount of carbon 14 and its relation to carbon 12, but they did not realize that their sample was not clean. They must sooner or later acknowledge that they made a big mistake and had an unsuspected contaminant. The longer they take to recognize that the date they obtained in 1988 was from a contaminated sample, the worse it is going to be.

Professor Mattingly does not think that the radiocarbon people can say much. For anyone to deny that exposed surfaces on this planet are not contaminated with microorganisms would be ludicrous. Microorganisms are everywhere. Mattingly believes that my hypothesis will be accepted, because the Shroud was undisturbed for so long a time. In spite of the mistake, he is willing to try cleaning the samples again, if we ever get Church authorization. And next time we will not use the wrong buffer!

•   •   •

Do you know what is going on inside the minds of the radiocarbon scientists now that they know they made a mistake? They are good scientists but only human. Respect them. Leave them alone. If they want to continue feeling the way they do, let them feel that way. If you are a scientist looking for the truth, this is one possibility. I have said in some of my conferences that if a person wants to be wrong, I will defend with my life his right to be wrong. Probably some of the radiocarbon people will go to the grave without accepting their mistake. But they did make a mistake.

Chapter 8

HOW WAS
THE IMAGE FORMED?

IF THE SHROUD IS AUTHENTIC, THERE MUST BE A SCIEN-
tific explanation for the formation of the image. Some people
have hypothesized that at the moment of Resurrection there was a
burst of radiation, with a release of thermal neutrons that "flashed"
the image onto the Shroud. But I cannot accept this; it is not science.
A body does not produce thermal neutrons. When I started to consider the Shroud seriously, I thought it would be authentic, because
there had never been a valid scientific explanation of the image. I
never believed that the Shroud was a painting, despite McCrone's
reports of pigments, since I knew the presence of iron oxide was a
common finding. Every ancient artifact has iron oxide on the surface
because of the deposit by bacteria, like the chemolithotrophs, that
oxidize iron to obtain energy with the deposit of iron oxide (hematite). So to me a deposit of iron oxide did not mean anything at all.
Paul Vignon, a scientist at the Catholic Institute in Paris at the beginning of the century, said that if the Shroud is authentic, there would
be a scientific explanation for the image. I accept that idea com-

pletely. I think that something physically present made the image and that good research will find it.

And I am convinced that my research has found the answer. I believe the image was formed by a relative deposit of bioplastic coating. (Remember that when I presented this idea at the CIELT in Rome in June of 1993, I lost most of my audience.) The areas that look darker on the positive image are the areas that had more natural deposits in the beginning with the dead body of Jesus of Nazareth, so the bacteria there grew faster than in the areas that had less contact with the body. If a part of the body was in direct contact with the textile, the concentration of sweat, salt, oils, blood, and urea was higher than where there was no direct contact. I repeat: those are the areas where the bacteria grew faster. I have seen this phenomenon in ancient Maya artifacts, with the presence of ancient blood and the presence of cotton fibers that, like the flax of the Shroud, were made of cellulose. It is directly related to the contact and concentration of human deposits. I am stating that the Shroud has a contact image. Those who say it is not a contact image are just guessing. One cannot cite as a scientific fact something one is merely speculating about. As I was told by my chemistry teachers in junior high, Professor Teodoro Liebana and Professor Manuel Hernandez Gaona at the Colegio Franco Mexicano (Marist Brothers) in Monterrey, Mexico, one must have the result before one can accept it.

I am convinced that the face was the first part of the image to be formed. Remember that the bacteria grow very slowly and only under particular conditions. I think the image was formed because the cloth was placed where it was under such particular conditions. There was the coincidence of all necessary factors working at the same time. Humidity, temperature, the bacteria being left alone to grow slowly in a particular position—all these were important factors. If you move the cloth, you will change the ecological balance, and the bacterial growth will also change. So the Shroud's being above a gate in Edessa for three hundred years, as suggested by Ian Wilson, would have provided ideal conditions. I have seen the same conditions in Maya jades. An artifact that has been handled a lot shows no form of image. But when you find a jade in a tomb that has been untouched for more than a thousand years, you will find this kind of image, the kind, I believe, that would take more than a hundred years to form.

The deposit is thicker in some areas of the Shroud because the blood in those places provided the bacteria with food material. Now this source of food has mostly been removed, and the bacteria have not grown at the same thickness over the whole area. I find this easy to understand, because I have seen the coating in many ancient artifacts. But the person who has not seen this type of natural deposit finds it difficult to accept. If you ask me why the same deposits were not produced in every area, I will answer that the growing conditions were different. This is a fact that I discovered while studying jades: in the areas with more organic deposit, the coating is thicker than in the areas without organic deposit. It is exactly this principle that applies to the Shroud.

Although the bacteria grow faster where there are large food deposits—for example, on blood from wounds—they will migrate over the whole area. That might lead one to expect that the image would be blurred. Yet the outlines are very distinct, not blurred. Why? I don't have the answer, but I do have the findings. They are in the speed of growth, the weight of the coating, and the feeding done on material found in the area. There are many factors. We know that water helps us when we are thirsty; we don't care about the scientific fact that it has two hydrogen atoms and one oxygen. We just use it. It is the same here: if a scientific finding repeats itself on different artifacts, one accepts it. Remember: Never argue with success.

Let us consider the Ahaw Pectoral. The pectoral, as we saw, comprised five pieces held together with cotton strings. With time, the strings were destroyed and eaten by the bacteria and fungi, but their image remains, as a kind of pseudomorph where they themselves were. The bacteria and fungi grew exactly at the places where the

cotton string was inside the pectoral. The bacteria did not grow between the fibers; it was as if they produced a mold around the fibers.
This is the phenomenon we saw in the Shroud: the bacteria grew only
where there were fibers.

My theory has been queried. It is said that if this is a contact
image, then wrapping the body should have produced a distorted
image, which is not what one sees on the Shroud. If you put powder
on strings and make an impression with them, you will have a distorted image. But if you let the bacteria work slowly over time, perhaps hundreds of years, you will have a perfect image. You must let
the bacteria do their work and make the deposits of iron oxide and
manganese oxide.

McCrone has said that he found more particulate matter in the
image areas than in non-image areas. I agree with him completely:
that is logical, and he is right. Some Shroudies say there is no deposit
on the image areas, but that is not science. I am more in agreement
with McCrone than with the Shroudies. I also totally disagree with
Dr. Adler's idea that the fibers show oxidative dehydration with corrosion. At a magnification of forty, you can see deposits even on non-
image fibers. The difference between a non-image area and an image
area is the thickness of the bioplastic coating; it is not that some areas
have no deposit or are corroded. A fiber from a modern linen has no
deposit at all, even when viewed under high magnification. Maybe the
"corrosion" Adler referred to was caused by the sticky tape. Maybe
parts of the fibers were eaten by the fungi and replaced by the bioplastic coating. But that would be guessing; it is not scientifically proven.

The plastic deposited by the bacteria has a composition of
polyhydroxyalkanoate (PHA), and some fungi love to eat this plastic.
In early 1993, when Father Cervantes and I were in Rome, I thought
some of the fungi I saw on other artifacts (Lichenothelia) had caused
the formation of the bioplastic coating. But the fungi do not produce
the plastic; they eat the plastic. I have been unable to culture the
fungus Lichenothelia from the Shroud threads. The strange thing is

that the *Leobacillus rubrus* produces an antifungal. The samples from the jades are covered almost completely with black fungi, but those fungi are not seen on the Shroud, because the bacteria that produce the plastic also produce an antifungal to defend against the fungi.

The STURP investigators used irradiation with specific wave lengths, and that method broke, or could have broken, the ecological balance of the bacteria. Once the balance is broken, some species of bacteria will grow faster than others and upset the balance. Then the image will start to become distorted. According to Riggi, the facial image is not what he remembers from 1978. When he looked at it again in 1988 as he was taking samples for the radiocarbon studies, he noticed a distortion. I have not talked with Riggi during the last three years, so I do not know how the image looked to him in the latest exhibition of the Shroud, from April 18 to June 14, 1998.

What could have happened to the body of Jesus of Nazareth after it was laid in the tomb? I don't know. All I can say is that the cloth was not in contact with the body for a long time, because there would have been signs of deterioration, as in any cloth used in the burial of a body. Our religion tells us that he resurrected at the third day, and I accept this teaching of the Church.

I believe that the image on the Shroud was not there at first but developed over time, as did the images on the jades. But where is the miracle? For me, the miracle in the production of the image on the Shroud is the presence of all the conditions necessary to form the image at the exact moment they were needed. Even if these conditions are explained scientifically, their presence at the precise moment they were needed for the production of the image may be interpreted as the miracle.

Chapter 9

"KNIGHTS OF THE ROUND TABLE"

N OT ONLY IS MY RESEARCH ALWAYS OPEN TO EVERY-
one, but I am eager to share it with fellow scientists and
with anyone who can offer suggestions and comments about it. After
the disappointing Rome symposium, where my concerns about com-
municating the importance of the bioplastic coating had fallen on
deaf ears, I was even more eager to share my findings with people
whose fields of expertise were close to mine. I was especially interested in talking to those actively involved in areas of research where I
was now treading, people like Walter McCrone, Alan Adler, and
Harry Gove in science, and, in history, Professor Daniel Scavone of
the University of Southern Indiana, with whom I shared many beliefs
about the history of the Shroud and its possible relation with the
Holy Grail. Accordingly, in September 1993 I organized the first of
three round tables, this one to be held, appropriately, at the University of Our Lady of the Lake, in San Antonio. Instead of throwing my
research to the wolves, as I had done in Rome, this time I hoped to get
considered and thoughtful reactions and suggestions. For that reason,

I tried to assemble a select group of qualified researchers who were interested in the Shroud and who could contribute to the round table discussion. Perhaps I would find out once and for all whether the evidence I had gathered would be compelling to an unbiased audience. I also wanted to learn about other types of research that were being done, since there might be information of mutual use that would answer some of my many questions. My hope was to have an enjoyable conference, with six to eight participants, in a comfortable atmosphere where everyone felt at ease in sharing information and in offering and receiving critical comments.

Walter McCrone came to our first round table and gave a paper on his theory that the Shroud was a painting. Alan Adler talked about his blood work on the Shroud samples of 1978 and about the Shroud's conservation. Professor Scavone, whom I had met by chance at New York's Kennedy Airport after the Rome symposium, talked on several important points in the history of the Shroud. We were joined by the President of the Society of Sindonology in Mexico, who came with Father Cervantes. Father Fred Brinkmann came as the representative of the Holy Shroud Guild in America.

I showed many slides from my research, each participant presented a paper, and after every paper we had a lengthy discussion of its pros and cons. I was particularly keen to know Walter McCrone's views on the bioplastic coating, because this conference was his first personal exposure to my ideas. Though I recalled reading McCrone's report on iron oxide in the journal *The Microscope* in 1980, I did not know much about his work until after I had talked with Adler in 1987. But in 1993, when my own research led to my interest in blood on ancient artifacts, I had got in touch with McCrone, and he had sent me copies of his journals of *Microscope,* vol. 28 and vol. 29. I had known that McCrone was wrong right from the beginning, but now I had proof.

McCrone said that there was iron oxide or red ochre in a gelatin-binding medium used by artists. I had found that yes, though there is iron oxide, which shows up as a reddish deposit, it was not pure hematite (another fancy name for iron oxide). It was hematite deposited by the bacteria that were using the energy of iron and manganese in order to thrive. All the artifacts I had been working with also had a blackish deposit of manganese oxide, and I knew about bacteria's use of energy from iron and manganese through my studies in chemistry and bacteriology. Even though McCrone did not accept my findings, he was always a perfect gentleman. I didn't ask him questions. He didn't ask me questions. We showed our respect for each other. (Remember my position: I will defend with my life his right to be wrong.) He gave me a big hug at the airport. He was happy that I had invited him, and he was very courteous.

The round table was Alan Adler's third exposure to the idea of the coating, because he had heard my paper in San Antonio in 1987 and in Rome in 1993. Adler looked through the microscope at my slides and said that I was right, that he had checked his fibers and found the bioplastic coating on them. He had acknowledged this from the start. Before coming to San Antonio, he had said there was no deposit, but after attending the meeting, he said that something was present. At times I found it difficult to talk with Adler. He could be correct in defining the blood, even though his arguments would not have stood up in court. The testing method he and John Heller were using for establishing the presence of blood is now outdated. For example, he was pushing the presence of hemoglobin because of the Soret band, a spectroscopic band. He and Heller said that the Soret band was specific to blood, but that is not correct. Many bacteria have cytochromes that absorb at this same band. The Soret band is not specific to blood, but the STURP scientists had enough certified information to prove that it was blood. I also told Adler that his theory of the production of the image by the oxidative dehydration of the image fibers is nonsense.

In November 1993, a small symposium was arranged in Mexico City by Father Cervantes, and Daniel Scavone and I were invited to present our research in history and in the bioplastic coating and blood. It was an excellent meeting; everybody was amiable and enjoyed the Mexican food and beer and on Sunday attended a Mass by Father Cervantes at the Cathedral of Mexico City.

After the first round table, in San Antonio, Daniel Scavone organized a meeting in Evansville, Indiana, on February 12, 1994. I immediately accepted the invitation, since one of my married daughters was living in Evansville, so my wife and I could visit her at the same time. At this meeting we were joined by Giovanni Riggi, making the first of three visits to the United States, partly to give a paper, partly to see the university.

Greatly encouraged by the first round table, I organized a second one to give the reports of the initial studies with the DNA from the Man on the Shroud. At this time I was Adjunct Professor of Microbiology at UTHSCSA and asked Mattingly to help me organize the round table in September 1994. I had specifically chosen this month because I had heard that Ian Wilson would then be in the States, but unfortunately he was unable to arrange his schedule to accommodate the meeting. Timothy Jull from the Arizona AMS facility was originally expected to attend but had to pull out at the last moment. Radiocarbon scientists, however, were well represented by Professor Harry Gove, a co-inventor of the accelerator mass spectrometry method for radiocarbon dating that had been used by the three laboratories in their attempts to date the Shroud.

I had become acquainted with Gove after reading the manuscript of his chapter for a book being edited by Paul Maloney, in Philadelphia. Maloney had sent me the manuscript with the approval of Gove. I then called Gove to see whether he wanted to read about my experience with radiocarbon dating of the Maya artifacts, and I subsequently sent him copies of my publications. That was the start of a useful dialogue and friendship. I know that he is an honest man, even though he had severe difficulties with Gonella in Turin. So I invited Gove to present a paper at the second round table and we got on very well. He is an easygoing man. Well, he was difficult with some of the Sturpies but not with me. He is not stubborn. If you prove your point, he will accept it.

When Gove arrived, I showed him a segment of a thread from the Shroud, and he was particularly interested in the coating he saw under the microscope, which was generally estimated to be a 60/40 percent ratio of bioplastic to linen. Scavone tried questioning Gove as he had questioned McCrone, but it is difficult for a scientist to be thrown off track. Even if Scavone was stubborn, he is a nice guy! He reported Gove's views in a letter to Ian Wilson, Editor of the British Society for the Turin Shroud's *Newsletter*. With Scavone's permission, it was published in the January 1995 edition of the *Newsletter*:

> *Dr. Harry Gove attended and was, albeit reluctantly, quite impressed with the work being done in Texas. After some lively debate during the informally designed Round Table and, later that evening, the observation of Shroud threads under the microscope, Gove said on Saturday, September 2, that he had observed what Garza had been asserting: that actual cellulose accounts for only 40% of a Shroud thread [sic for fiber], the bioplastic coating accounting for 60%. What the laboratories dated, therefore, will have been the recent accretions of micro-organic life, and the hard coating they form, more so than pure Shroud linen.*

When the *Newsletter* appeared, Gove was upset because he did not yet want his views published. He was in a difficult position, because it looked as though he was throwing dirt at the rest of the radiocarbon group. He needed to make things more balanced, so he asked that a short statement be published in the next edition of the *Newsletter*. In the May 1995 issue he backtracked a little:

> I am afraid that Dan Scavone may have read too much into comments I made about the findings of Dr. Garza-Valdes . . .
>
> It may be that the "bioplastic coating" will change the Shroud date somewhat. My bet is that it is unlikely to do so by more than a hundred years or so—but time will tell . . . Those of us who attended this round table were convinced of the general validity of Garza-Valdes' findings: there was some sort of "halo" or bioplastic coating around some of the threads [sic for fibers]. I have been wrongly quoted . . . as saying my visual inspection through a microscope of some of Garza-Valdes' Shroud threads indicated that as much as 60% of this was bioplastic coating.

But Scavone was right. Gove had admitted that in front of me. He doesn't yet accept the degree of coating because he is human. One has to respect scientists; they are not toys. You cannot play with them. I have never pushed McCrone or Adler, and I think I am a friend of all of them, even though I was told by Judith Wilson in an E-mail that many Shroudies did not like my Shroud research.

At the end of the session I felt that Gove was an honest person who acknowledged that the carbon dating was wrong. I respect him, and he respects me. He has been honest with me, and he knows that I have been honest with him. So there is no problem. We communicate two or three times a week. We meet in New York and have a good time. We enjoy a Scotch and soda, and meet socially. We communicate by E-mail and phone, and it is to his great credit that he has agreed to head another series of radiocarbon-dating runs on ancient artifacts. Whether the Shroud will be included in this series is out of our hands.

We recently published together the results of tests on an Egyptian ibis mummy. They show a big difference between the radiocarbon age of the bird bones and tissue and the age of the linen wrappings of the mummy—a difference of 550 years, as we shall see in the next chapter.

Chapter 10

PROBLEMS
WITH MUMMIES . . .

J

UST AS I HAD BEEN FORTUNATE ENOUGH TO BE ABLE TO
buy the Itzamna Tun and the Ahaw Pectoral when I was in my
twenties, I was able to enrich my now-widening interest in possible
radiocarbon dating anomalies by acquiring a mummy. What I needed
was an artifact that had a clear discrepancy between the dating of the
body and its wrappings.

God acts in different ways, as my good friend Father Cervantes
used to say. I received in the post a catalogue from a New York
auction house, Harmer Rooke Galleries, with which I had had deal-
ings in the past. And there in the catalogue was just what I had been
looking for: an ibis mummy! There aren't all that many crazy people
buying Egyptian mummies. It was not too expensive—a few thousand
dollars for a mummy that is four thousand years old! As the cult
animal of the god Thoth, the ibis was sacred to the Egyptians. At
temples like the one of Thoth at Hermopolis, the birds were bred and
generally pampered. Pilgrims would buy them and have them mummified as offerings to the god, and they would then be buried, by the
thousands, in vast underground necropolises. Bulls and other animals

also considered sacred by the Egyptians were mummified and buried the same way. How my mummy came to end up in a New York auction house was anyone's guess. I bought it over the telephone at the end of December 1995, after the second round table and before the third, which I was organizing for January 26–27, 1996. The ibis mummy became affectionately known as Danny the Mummy, after Professor Dan Scavone, and was to be the star of the January meeting.

Another star of this third round table was Dr. Rosalie David, head of the Department of Egyptology at the Manchester Museum, England. In fact, it was she who had prompted my search for a mummy. About ten years earlier, I had bought her book *Mysteries of the Mummies*, but to be honest, I had not yet read it. When I hit the problem of the anomaly in dating my Maya artifacts, I found her book in my library and learned that she had had a problem dating a mummy in the Manchester collection, called Mummy 1770. It was of a thirteen-year-old girl, and had been excavated by the famous Egyptologist Sir Flinders Petrie, back in the 1890s.

When Dr. David and her colleagues carefully and scientifically unwrapped this mummy in 1975, they sent samples from the bones and the wrappings to the British Museum for radiocarbon dating. The datings for two types of samples were widely divergent. The bones were found to be from c. 1510 B.C., but the mummy's wrappings were much younger, c. A.D. 255; a difference of more than fifteen hundred years. These weird findings left Dr. David with two possible scenarios. The first was that the mummy's body had been rewrapped all those years after her death and burial. But the second, which was of more interest to me, was that some form of contamination—Dr. David speculated about something in the resins and unguents used for the mummification process—had interfered with the correct radiocarbon dating. There was also a possible error, acknowledged by the British Museum laboratory, that might have affected the dating of the samples.

Once I finished reading her book, I got in touch with Dr. David because I thought I had the answer to her problem: the radiocarbon-dating results again had been skewed by the presence of a bioplastic coating. Dr. David was receptive to the idea and suggested that I study samples from Mummy 1770. At the time, we were organizing the First International Archaeomicrobiology Symposium, to be held at the University of Texas Health Science Center on January 26, 1996. This was the first time the term *archaeomicrobiology* had been used, covering the ecology, taxonomy, and the secondary metabolites produced by microorganisms colonizing the surface of ancient artifacts. We intended to run this in tandem with the third round table, to be held on January 27. Since Dr. David was a natural choice for both meetings, I invited her, and she enthusiastically agreed to change her schedule so that she could attend the meetings. Of the seven papers presented, two were given by Dr. David to an audience of approximately forty delegates, many of them archaeologists and many of them scientists. I had hoped to get samples of Mummy 1770 to examine under the microscope, and Dr. David happily obliged. There it was, a beautiful bioplastic coating present on the bandages that had been used to wrap the mummy! When I showed Dr. David the Shroud samples, we talked about the coating on both artifacts. According to Dr. David, that was a breakthrough. She felt that there was one cause for the dating problems of both objects, and she promised to organize a symposium in Manchester to discuss it further. So far, it has not taken place.

When I brought out Danny the Mummy for her inspection, she saw that it had never before been unwrapped and would therefore be an excellent example for further testing of the radiocarbon system. At one-thirty that Saturday afternoon, Dr. David gave samples of the wrappings and of the bone to Dr. Douglas Donahue of the AMS laboratory in Arizona, so that he could submit them to radiocarbon dating. What he got were samples of linen wrappings, one part cleaned by the acid-base-acid technique and another cleaned first with acetone and then with the acid-base-acid. Dr. Donahue was also given a bone segment of the bird and some muscle tissue near the bone.

The support of Dr. Rosalie David was not the only benefit from this third round table. The second round table had been attended by one of the original members of the STURP team, Dr. Robert Dinegar, who at the time of the 1978 testing had been attached to the National Scientific Research Laboratory at Los Alamos. He was now with the University of New Mexico in Los Alamos. On January 5, 1996, I had received a fax saying that he had enjoyed being at the second round table, and would appreciate an invitation to attend the third one later that month. Of course I was delighted to invite him.

During the second round table, Dinegar had been eager to talk to Dr. Gove, but Gove had kept his distance. I learned later that the radiocarbon scientists felt Dinegar had been "pushy," trying to control their research. At this third meeting, Dr. Dinegar admitted that when he had first looked at samples from the Shroud with the optical microscope, back in 1978, he had seen the coating that interested me, but had been told by a senior member of the STURP team to shut up! I quote Dr. Dinegar:

> *I'm happy that you're showing these pictures, because I've seen the same type of coating on the tapes taken by Rodgers in 1978. When I pointed out the presence of the coating on the fibers, I was told by other members of STURP to close my mouth.*

Dinegar, in fact, named the senior STURP member who had called him down, but I will leave it to those of you who know the Shroudie world to fill the gap. This news, naturally, disappointed me. I had always had my doubts about STURP, but now I thought, "This is not science."

Once the third round table was over, we eagerly awaited the

radiocarbon-dating results on Danny the Mummy. Because the samples had been delivered by Dr. David directly to Dr. Donahue, the
results were to go to her, even though Dr. Donahue knew I owned the
mummy and had organized the symposium. (Is this another episode in
which a Chichimec Mexican Indian is not as important as a Euro-
pean?) Dr. Gove also received the results a couple of months later and
kindly gave me a copy. Once again, there was a significant discrepancy between the age of the bird and the age of the wrappings! It was
an average of 550 years, yet another example of an anomalous radiocarbon-dating outcome. I had said to Dr. Gove before the testing that
I would feel my theory vindicated if there was a difference of anything
over five hundred years, because I had found the coating on the ibis to
be much thinner than the coating on the Shroud fibers, even though
the mummy was older. I am now sorry that I did not bet Gove a pair
of cowboy boots, as he had done with his assistant, Shirley Brignall,
back in 1988, over the Shroud result! Seriously, I felt that the radiocarbon-dating method had been shown to be faulty because it had
failed to take the bioplastic coating into account. But once again the
radiocarbon group wriggled to refute this claim. I was now told that
the ibis was probably a bad choice of subject because it could have
lived on fish from the sea! As we saw earlier, when discussing the
basic principles of radiocarbon dating, the relationship of carbon 14
to carbon 12 may be different in the case of marine fish, which thrive
on plants from the bottom of the sea. Therefore, anything feeding on
these fish, like Danny the Mummy, could itself have an altered carbon
14 content. There could, of course, have been a "marine correction"
applied to the figures. Timothy Jull of the Arizona laboratory said he
had been told to mention this idea of the diet, but since he personally
did not believe it, he had not passed it along. (He is a good scientist,
and, as I will explain later, the delta 13 of the sample indicates that
no correction was needed.) Rosalie David said if, as was likely, Danny
the Mummy came from the Thoth temple at Hermopolis in Middle
Egypt, he would have had to do a daily round trip of five hundred

miles to get his fish from the Mediterranean Sea and then swim to the bottom of the sea to eat them! Dr. Rosalie David, Dr. Gove, Dr. Mattingly, and I have stated that we do not believe this.

I have had no further communication with Dr. Donahue since 1996. I am glad that he attended the third round table. But he was in a weak position, since he felt the environment to be hostile. I am sorry about that. His comment, after he saw my presentation at the meeting of the bioplastic coating, was "We shall see." But it is not a matter of choice; that is the point. He saw the coating for himself.

Where do we go from here? Do we keep testing and testing? Gove has suggested testing samples from a mummified bull in the Smithsonian Museum in Washington. We could run the test on as many animals as possible, but the results will always be the same. I don't know why we keep looking and looking. We have already tested the Shroud, Mummy 1770, the Maya Itzamna Tun, and Danny the Mummy. Every case has produced that abnormal result. There is not a single case in my research that has been normal. The Shroud of Turin result was abnormal because of the bioplastic coating. The Mummy 1770 result was abnormal because of the bioplastic coating. The Itzamna Tun result was abnormal because of the bioplastic coating. And Danny the Mummy had the coating, and the result was wrong. Why do we continue to look? I am happy with the results we now have. So is Dr. Rosalie David. If others want to continue looking, let them, but they will not find a difference. I am convinced that at the present time, the radiocarbon dating of ancient textiles is not a reliable test.

Chapter 11

EVEN MORE
PROBLEMS
WITH CARDINALS...

FOLLOWING THE SUCCESSFUL CLONING OF THE THREE gene segments from the samples of blood on the Shroud, I sent a fax to Cardinal Saldarini, telling him of our success. I received no acknowledgment. The first indication I had of trouble was when I heard that Cardinal Saldarini had issued a statement following "recently published press reports concerning the Holy Shroud."

The gist was that

> . . . while the Church recognized every scientist's right to carry out research that he feels to be suitable in his field of science, in this case it is necessary to point out that:
>
> a) no new sample of material has been taken from the Holy Shroud since 21 April 1988, and, as far as the Custodian of the Holy Shroud knows, there is no residual material from that sample in the hands of third parties;
>
> b) if such material exists, the Custodian reminds everybody that the Holy See has not given permission to anybody to keep it and do what he wants with it. The Custodian

*requests those concerned to give the piece back to the Holy
See;*

*c) as there is no degree of certainty about whether the
material in question on which these aforesaid experiments
have been carried out actually comes from the fabric of the
Shroud, the Holy See and the Papal Custodian declare that
they cannot recognize any serious value in the results of the
alleged experiments.*

The statement, dated September 1995, clearly seemed to be directed toward my research, research I had always assumed to be bona
fide, thanks to my samples having been given to me by a person I
believed had full Church authority to pass them on. From my understanding of what Luigi Gonella had told me, the samples had been
preserved on the authority of Cardinal Ballestrero, to be utilized in
future "honest" research if they were required. How was I to know
that I had been caught in a political situation in which the words of
Cardinal Ballestrero would be disregarded once he relinquished his
custodianship of the Shroud to Cardinal Saldarini, as happened in
September 1990? When I obtained the samples in Turin in May 1993,
I had no way of knowing about this difference of opinion between the
two Cardinals. I believed that Riggi and Gonella had the authority to
give me the samples. There seems to be a difference between what
Cardinal Ballestrero said recently and what he said in 1988. That is
politics, and I do not intend to become involved in it. But I do not
think that Gonella is the power behind the Cardinal that he was
during Ballestrero's regime, and I do not know whether anyone has
taken his place. As far as I can tell, three people behave as if they have
the position: Don Giuseppe Ghiberti, Dr. Bruno Barberis, and Dr.
Pierre Luigi Baima-Bollone.

Were the samples from Riggi truly from the Shroud of Turin? I
have the photograph of Luigi Gonella and Riggi's seals on the con-

tainer in which the samples were kept. There is no doubt, as one looks at the samples, that they are from the Shroud. Also, during my conference at the Polytechnic of Turin, where I showed the photographs of the samples, Dr. Franco A. Testore, who had actually done the weighing of the Shroud segments, recognized the three trimmings as being from the borders of the segment cut on April 21, 1988. Dr. Franco A. Testore is a professor at the Polytechnic University in Turin, and Director of the university's Textile Department. Does Cardinal Saldarini think that I am a dishonest person and that I changed the samples? Or are there intense political intrigues behind all this that I do not know, nor in which I care to be involved?

I sent a faxed copy of every single report to Cardinal Saldarini. A phone conversation with his personal secretary, Don Luciano Morello, confirms that the Cardinal received my reports. I faxed our findings of human male blood only a week after I had the result. I received no answer from him until the upsetting letter of 1996. That was three years after my initial report.

In the spring of 1996, the University Health Science Center at San Antonio published its journal, *The Mission,* featuring a major article about my research on both my Maya artifacts and the Shroud of Turin, as well as the results of the DNA testing. On the front cover was the facial image of Christ as seen on the Shroud, with the caption: "Secrets of the Shroud—Microbiologists discover how the Shroud of Turin hides its true age." The article, written by Jim Barrett, outlined my hypothesis about the bioplastic coating and covered the work that had been done with Rosalie David's Mummy 1770. It also reported the findings of human blood by Dr. Tryon's Center for Advanced DNA Technologies. It said, in part, "After months examining microscopic samples, the team concluded in January that the Shroud of Turin is centuries older than its carbon date." Dr. Harry Gove was quoted as saying, "This is not a crazy idea." Having heard nothing from Cardinal Saldarini in response to the various faxes and reports I had sent to keep him informed about my research, I sent him a copy of the magazine.

It was probably the magazine that finally elicited a response from Cardinal Saldarini. His letter, dated July 31, 1996, and written in Italian, was translated for me by Dr. Roberto Rolfini, and it upset me greatly. In it, the Cardinal asked "by whose authority" I had done my work. In reply, I sent Cardinal Saldarini a copy of the letter I had received from His Holiness John Paul II back in April 1994, with my comment: "By this authority." Perhaps it was not the most diplomatic response, given the circumstances . . .

The Cardinal also accused me of not having respect for the millions who believe that the blood on the Shroud is from Jesus. (In other words, he was asking me to hide the truth.) He asked how it was possible for me to report that we had done studies on the blood from the Shroud. I am a Catholic; I studied for eleven years in a Catholic school (Colegio Franco Mexicano in Monterrey). I see no problem with any of the studies we did. I think that the Cardinal does not understand. And he said that, since the samples had not been given to me officially by the Church, the Church cannot recognize my research on the Shroud. Again, I say that I was dealing with the man I believed to be the official representative of the Church—and with samples contained in a parcel officially sealed by a signatory of the Church.

So what is my present relation with Giovanni Riggi? Communications are sparse. Until June 1998, I used to talk by phone with Luigi Gonella at least once a month and ask him to keep Riggi informed. In June 1998 I talked with Gonella for the last time. He informed me that he was having political headaches in Turin because of my research and would prefer that I keep my distance from him. I will always acknowledge the favor he and Riggi did for me. After Riggi realized that we made a mistake in cleaning the Shroud samples, he was so upset that he broke off relations. As for Gonella himself, perhaps because he was not present when we studied the trimmings and the tapes in Turin, he has never ever been particularly enthusiastic about my research. (Sometimes I wonder whether, on our initial trip to Turin in 1993, it was Riggi who initiated the visit to us at the Hotel Sitea or whether the visit was suggested by Gonella). Although Gonella is somewhat ambivalent, he tends to believe that the Shroud is probably not authentic. Now he is between the wall and the sword . . .

For me, the subject is finished. There are people I will never be able to convince, but I respect them. Adler will never change his views. Donahue will never change his views. McCrone will never change his views. And it has never been my intention to change their opinions. I simply have been trying to find the truth. I did the research because I was interested in the bioplastic coating and, after my confrontation with those so-called New York connoisseurs, thought the best way to solve the problem was to learn all I could about the weathering of ancient artifacts. If the others choose to accept my research, that's all right. If they didn't want to accept it, that's all right, too. We can respect everyone's opinions. We live in a free society and do not try to force anyone to agree with our ideas. My responsibility as a scientist is to report my findings. When, as a physician, I offer a patient my diagnosis, I give him advice and suggest what might effect a cure. But I cannot force him to get better. If he does not choose to take the prescribed medicine, he is free to do that. But he should not call me at 2:00 A.M. to tell me that he hasn't improved.

Everything can be so open and beautiful and clean. I don't understand why some people try to make it difficult.

Chapter 12

THE
SWAN SONG

O N SUNDAY, JUNE 21, 1998 (FATHER'S DAY), CARDI-
nal Anastasio Ballestrero died in Italy. All his life, Cardinal
Ballestrero had tried to defend the Shroud. Ten years ago, he was
forced for political reasons to accept the radiocarbon tests. How difficult it must have been for him at the press conference that Thursday,
October 13, 1988, when he reported the medieval age (1260–1390)
of the Shroud. With his death, a golden age of Shroud research came
to an end. The previous week, the fourth exhibition of the Shroud in
this century had just finished. (The Shroud was on exhibit from April
18 to June 14, 1998.) I am unhappy that the Shroud research I carried
out between 1993 and 1998 was not recognized by Cardinal Saldarini
or by Don Giuseppe Ghiberti during Cardinal Ballestrero's life.

I tried to keep Cardinal Ballestrero informed of all my scientific
findings on the Shroud, even though he was in retirement. He knew
that some scientists did not accept the medieval age date given to the
flax fibers of the textile from the Shroud of Turin on October 13,
1988.

I was in Turin for the opening of the 1988 exhibit. How painful for me were the words of Cardinal G. Saldarini *("Non e una reliquia, ma un' icona che rappresenta la passione di Cristo, un mistero che porta i nostri occhi a Cristo")* during the homily of the Missa Solemnis of the Holy Shroud at 4:00 P.M. in the Cathedral of St. John the Baptist on Saturday, April 18, 1998. Thanks to the courtesy of Professor Bruno Barberis, I was close to the Cardinal (less than ten meters) during Mass, and his words still reverberate in my ears. I could not believe that they came from the Official Keeper of the Shroud: "It is not a relic but an icon that represents the passion of Christ, a mystery that transports our eyes to Christ." How different from the words of His Holiness John Paul II, reported by O. Petrosillo, when His Holiness concelebrated a Mass in Turin on April 13, 1980. The Pope declared the Shroud a Turin treasure: "an unusual and mysterious relic like the Holy Shroud." Petrosillo also reported that on April 28, 1989, during a flight to Madagascar with His Holiness John Paul II, he asked His Holiness, "Is the Shroud an icon or a relic?" The Pope answered: "Certainly it is a relic; it could not be changed. If it were not a relic, these acts of faith that surround it and that also show themselves more strongly than the evidences—than the counterevidence of scientific order—could not be understood."

Petrosillo also mentioned that when he and E. Marinelli gave a copy of the Polish translation of their book to His Holiness, he said, "It is very important to maintain the apostolate through the Shroud. Because the Lord left it to us close to the sacraments."

Thanks to the courtesy of Professor Piero Savarino, I had the opportunity that same day, April 18, 1998, before Mass, to study the Shroud for more than an hour at a distance of five meters. I examined the images at leisure. The impression I gained from the images on the cloth was that of the presence of multiple stains forming the figure, and not the presence of a manmade painting.

In his book *A Doctor at Calvary,* P. Barbet mentioned that, in 1942, J. Volckringer, a pharmacist at St. Joseph's Hospital in Paris, reported the development of naturally formed images of botanical

remnants (flowers and leaves) when these specimens were stored between the pages of books or notebooks. The images appeared on the
paper (cellulose) only in those cases in which the herbal remnants had
been in storage for more than a hundred years. The images were
formed by the natural production of multiple stains, similar to the
stains that composed the images on the cellulose of the fibers of the
Shroud. And these herbal images had the same photographic negative
character as the images on the Shroud.

After the Missa Solemnis of the Holy Shroud, I had the opportunity to shake hands with Cardinal Giovanni Saldarini and introduce
myself. The day before, April 17, 1998, I had given a copy of the
third draft of the manuscript of this book to Don Luciano Morello,
Cardinal Saldarini's personal secretary, whom I had met five years
earlier, in May 1993. I told him the findings of the wooden tubules
(from an angiosperm or hardwood) mixed with the blood from the
occipital area on the dorsal image of the Man on the Shroud. I explained to Don Morello the importance of these findings, which indicate that the patibulum of the True Cross was made not of pine
(gymnosperm or softwood), as was believed, but from oak. Don Morello insisted that I report my findings about the wooden remnants at
the International Congress of Sindonology, to be held in Turin from
June 5 until June 7, 1998.

After three days in Turin, I returned to San Antonio to continue my
medical practice and to make plans to go to Turin for the meeting in
June. A week after I got back to San Antonio, I received a fax from
Dr. Testore, inviting me to give a lecture at the Polytechnic University
on June 5, before the start of the Congress of Sindonology. Dr. Testore had been present at the taking of the samples from the Shroud on
April 21, 1988, and was in charge of recording the weights of the
various segments cut for the radiocarbon studies.

Several months earlier, I had submitted for consideration an abstract of a paper I wanted to present at the congress but I did not

receive an answer from the organization committee (read P. L. Baima-Bollone). I decided to phone Baima-Bollone, who was the president and organizer and who decided on the presentations. He asked me to submit a new abstract and offered me five minutes in which to make my oral presentation. After sending the new abstract, I called again. This time Baima-Bollone told me I would have ten minutes to give my paper.

Having accepted Dr. Testore's invitation to give a lecture at the university, on June 5, 1998, I presented "The Microbiology of the Shroud of Turin." After the lecture I was invited by Dr. Testore for lunch at a restaurant near the university, where I ate one of the best pastas that I remember. I thought I was a good eater, but in this case Dr. Testore won the match.

In the afternoon we went to the opening of the congress in the building of the International Industrial Union. The President of the Republic of Italy and His Excellency Cardinal Giovanni Saldarini, Archbishop of Turin, were present for the start of the activities.

The scientific sessions began that same evening, Friday, June 5, 1998. The President of the Republic and His Excellency the Cardinal left before the reports were given. Immediately after the initiation of activities, there was a difference of opinion between the French and the Italians. When A. Upinsky was presenting his paper, *"Le statut scientifique du Linceul du Turin: authentication officielle et descriptage,"* he ran out of time. The president of the meeting, Professor Pierre Luigi Baima-Bollone, asked Upinsky to stop. Upinsky ignored Baima-Bollone and said that he would finish his presentation. Baima-Bollone then asked that the light for the projector that Upinsky was using and the microphone both be disconnected. Upinsky continued talking without the microphone, and some of those in the audience started whistling. It was an extremely uncomfortable situation. The whistling reminded me of an episode fifty years earlier, during my childhood in Monterrey, when a movie at a neighborhood cinema was suddenly interrupted by the projectionist. Immediately, people began whistling and calling the projectionist nasty names. The episode during A. Upinsky's presentation was an example of the tone of the congress.

The next day, Saturday, June 6, I was to present my paper, "The Oak of Golgotha," at the morning session. But Baima-Bollone unexpectedly skipped over the three speakers who had been scheduled before me and, instead, called me to the podium. Not knowing quite what to make of this, I calmly went ahead with my presentation. After I was done, Baima-Bollone asked Don Giuseppe Ghiberti to read an unscheduled paper. In it, Cardinal Giovanni Saldarini declared my research to be officially invalid. Later, I tried more than a dozen times to speak with Father Ghiberti on the phone, but he never returned my calls. The Shroud samples that I had studied are the three trimmings removed by Riggi and Testore; and they are authentic. I did not realize that, at the end of the twentieth century, some people still hope to nullify scientific findings with political declarations. But I am glad, at least, that the Inquisition is no longer in power. If it does come back, I would probably be even more unlucky than Galileo in 1663; he was merely silenced, but I might be burned at the stake.

I know that my writing this book may bring about the end of my studies on the Shroud of Turin, but I must report my research and my findings in an honest way, even though this might be my swan song.

Chapter 13

THE OAK
OF GOLGOTHA

O F ALL THE EVENTS SURROUNDING THE PASSION OF
Jesus of Nazareth, none has been so closely contemplated
as the Crucifixion. Much has been speculated about the exact circumstances of Jesus' Crucifixion, but aside what the Gospel accounts tell
us (and there is considerable debate about their accuracy), there has
been almost nothing that could be declared with certainty about what
happened in Jesus' final hours. As my research on the Shroud continued, I held on to the hope that some clues would present themselves,
particularly in regard to the circumstances of the Crucifixion.

Capital punishment was common in ancient times, and crucifixion, its cruelest form, was one of the methods most frequently employed. The condemned person was bound or nailed to a tree or a
cross and was left to die. This highly visible, protracted mode of
execution was thought to be a more effective deterrent than other
methods.

Ancient Persians, Assyrians, and Greeks all regularly practiced
some form of this punishment, but the practice has been especially
identified with the Romans, who resorted to it extensively throughout

their empire, usually as punishment for those committing high trea-
son, for disobedient slaves, and for violent criminals. To show the
extent to which it was employed, we can point out that in one instance during the first century B.C., the Romans crucified six thousand
rebellious slaves who had participated in the revolt led by Spartacus.
The historian Josephus also reported that Titus ordered the crucifixion of five hundred Jews each day during his siege of Jerusalem. But
crucifixion was not entirely unknown before the Romans' arrival,
since Jewish law stipulated that the corpse of a man executed for a sin
worthy of death was to be hanged on a tree to show that he was
accursed of God (Deut. 21:22–23).

The full penalty of Roman crucifixion would typically begin with
the condemned being flogged and then being forced to carry the *patibulum* to the site of his execution. There, entirely naked, the man
would be nailed to the bar he had carried, which would be attached
to the vertical *stipes* set in the ground. The patibulum usually had a
mortise carved in the middle to hold the tenon of the stipes, complet-
ing the juncture. Aside from these basic elements, there was no set
procedure, and much depended on the executioner's decision about
how badly the condemned was to suffer. Since there seldom were
immediately mortal injuries inflicted, death came slowly, sometimes
even after several days of atrocious pain. After the executed man died,
his body would be left on the cross for days as an example.

Because of the large number of crucifixions the Roman soldiers
carried out, they used whatever wood was at hand, though timber
was fairly scarce. At that time, the oak was the most common tree in
Palestine. For that reason, many have theorized that Jesus was crucified upon a cross made of oak, but there is no evidence, from eyewit-
ness accounts or physical clues, to support that idea.

Throughout history, numerous people have claimed to own pieces
of the True Cross or of some other artifact from the site of the Crucifixion of Jesus at Golgotha. A patibulum at the Basilica of the Holy
Cross in Jerusalem, in Lateran, Rome, is believed to be from the cross

of the Good Thief, who was crucified alongside Jesus. This patibulum has the mortise described previously, but, as I will explain later, it is not of the correct dimensions.

In the pieces of Scotch tape used by Riggi to lift the blood samples from the occipital area of the Man on the Shroud, the several wood tubules I found were from an oak, indicating, clearly, that if the Shroud is authentic, the patibulum carried by Jesus of Nazareth on his way to Golgotha was of oak.

Chapter 14

HIS HOLINESS
JOHN PAUL II

O F COURSE, AFTER THE FIASCO AT THE JUNE 1998 International Congress, I couldn't help feeling that things would begin to improve. Certainly it was discouraging to hear Don Ghiberti read a document from the Church authorities declaring my studies unofficial. That was exacerbated by the person who came to me afterward to say that my samples were not authentic, even though this person had never seen them. These and other experiences made me hesitant to trust anyone about the scientific aspects of the Shroud. I was reminded of the pre-Columbian art "connoisseurs" who told me my jades were fake.

In December of 1993 I had sent to His Holiness John Paul II a copy of my "Bioplastic Coating on the Shroud of Turin: A Preliminary Report." So I decided to give him a draft of the manuscript of this book, containing the findings of the last five years. Ideally, I wanted to present the manuscript in person. I believed that such an opportunity would be a positive step forward in my study of the Shroud.

I explained my lofty hopes to Father John A. Leies, who knew people in Rome who might be able to arrange an audience with the Pope. We learned that His Holiness would be on vacation at Castel Gandolfo the week I had planned on going to Rome, but that he would grant limited audiences on Sundays at Castel Gandolfo and on Wednesdays at the Paul VI Audience Hall, in Vatican City. This limitation on his availability did not bode well for my getting in to see him.

I have been an optimistic person all my life, so it is not surprising that, even without a scheduled audience, I decided to go to Rome. We left on Thursday, July 23, 1998, and established ourselves at the Aldrovandi Palace Hotel at the Villa Borghese. On Saturday I went to the Prefettura Della Casa Pontificia and entered through the Bernini bronze doors at the right end of the colonnade. (It is the main entrance to the Apostolic Palace.) I gave two copies of the manuscript of *The DNA of God?* to Brother John Baldwin, who suggested that I try to give a copy to His Holiness during the audience in the Paul VI Audience Hall on the following Wednesday. I wrote out the formal request, which was channeled to the right authorities.

Even if I were able to enter the audience, there was no guarantee that I would be allowed to greet His Holiness directly. The hall has a capacity of nine thousand people, and there are four thousand pilgrims on average received during the Wednesday audience. Of these four thousand, there are only fifty places at the *prima fila* reserved for those who are to greet the Pope directly and shake hands with him. With the same optimism that brought me to Rome, I requested two of those fifty seats. I was told that if the invitation was granted, it would be delivered to my hotel on Tuesday afternoon.

After this stop, I went to the Basilica of the Holy Cross in Jerusalem, in Lateran, Rome, where there are several relics of the Passion of Christ and the patibulum of the cross of the Good Thief. The relics of the Passion of Christ are stored in the Chapel of the Relics, at the left of the main nave of the church. As soon as one enters the Chapel of the Relics, one sees the patibulum of the cross of the Good Thief, which is 1.78 meters in length, 13 centimeters wide and has a thickness of 8 centimeters. The mortise is in the center of the wide face of the patibulum (wrong side for the mortise) and has a diameter of 3 centimeters. I immediately noted that the hole's diameter was too small to be easily united with the tenon of the stipes after the prisoner had been nailed and the patibulum lifted to the upper part of the stipes. The clear impracticality of this gave me many doubts about the authenticity of this relic.

The entrance to the second room of the Chapel of the Relics had been constructed in a shape of a cross by Florestano Di Fausto at the beginning of the present century. The relics of the Passion of Christ, displayed in a large glass compartment, are (a) three wooden segments from the True Cross, (b) a segment of the Titulus used on the Cross with the INRI inscription, (c) a nail used in the Crucifixion of Jesus of Nazareth, (d) two thorns from the Crown of Thorns, (e) fragments of the Holy Sepulcher and of the column of the flagellation of Jesus of Nazareth, and (f) the right-hand index finger of St. Matthew. I studied these grisly relics carefully, taking several close-up photographs, looking for whatever clues I could find to their origins. But I began to wonder whether I was doing the correct thing. Who was I to try to prove or disprove scientifically the authenticity of these relics? My research began fifteen years ago when I tried to find a scientific way of proving the age of ancient Maya artifacts. Now, I had unleashed myself, as it were, to examine every relic of faith under the sun. By studying these Christian relics, I was following a quicksand path, and before I realized it, I had sunk up to my neck.

After the visit to the Basilica of the Holy Cross we went to the Plaza Navona, where charcoal portraits were drawn of our grandchildren, Sophia and Alexander, who had accompanied us to Rome. The drawings were followed by a dinner of fettuccini and Frascatti wine at the same restaurant where the late Father Cervantes and I had had dinner in June of 1993 while being serenaded with the song "Arrivederci Roma."

On Sunday we went to Ostia to swim in the sea. The beach was beautiful, but the sand was so hot that we could not walk on it barefooted. Several Roman mermaids—topless swimmers—were swimming, which only called the attention to intruders like us. One of these voluptuous mermaids came out of the water about two meters from where I stood, and suddenly she was in front of me. Sophia, my six-year-old granddaughter, was nearby. She looked up at me and asked, "Grandpa, why do you look so pale?"

On the next day, Monday, we went to the Basilica of Santa Maria Maggiore. If the Basilica of the True Cross is a "Jerusalem," the Basilica of Santa Maria Maggiore is a "Bethlehem." In this church is the relic of the crib of the infant Jesus. The Basilica of Santa Maria Maggiore was built at the highest point of the Esquiline Hill, one of the Seven Hills of Rome. When you enter the central nave of Santa Maria Maggiore, you immediately see a *baldacchino,* a canopy, at the main altar similar to, though not as big as, the one in St. Peter's Basilica. Above the baldacchino is a large mosaic described as the "Triumphal Arch of Ephesus." It is the triumphal arch built to celebrate the Ecumenical Council in Ephesus. Built in A.D., 440, it is the oldest mosaic in the basilica.

One of the side chapels caught my attention, the Chapel of St. Catherine of Alexandria, also known as the Cesi Chapel. The painting of St. Catherine above the altar is the depiction of the Crucifixion of Christ in a Tau cross, or *crux commissa.*

On Tuesday morning we went to the Church of Santa Sabina to take photographs of the fifth-century panel of the crucifixion in one of the church's main doors. The panel, one of the earliest representations of the Crucifixion of Jesus, is a wooden carving of Christ with his arms extended, and, beside him, the two thieves with their arms extended. But none of the three crosses is represented.

After lunch, I went to the hotel to see whether the invitation for the general audience with His Holiness had showed up and whether Fortune had smiled on me with seats in the *prima fila.* I didn't have to wait long; around two o'clock the invitation for the audience *and* the *prima fila* arrived. What a relief! I would be able to place a copy of my manuscript of *The DNA of God?* in the hands of His Holiness.

Wednesday morning at eight, my wife, Maria del Socorro, and I were at the entrance of the Paul VI Audience Hall in Vatican City. We were directed to the *prima fila,* where we enjoyed the singing and music of the pilgrim groups that had come from all over the world; there were more than four thousand pilgrims. A large group from Mexico, displaying a huge Mexican flag, was singing, *"Juan Pablo Segundo! Te quiere todo el mundo!"*

His Holiness slowly walked into the auditorium at nine-thirty. My first impression was that he seemed very tired. Pope John Paul II is not an old man; he was born on May 18, 1920. And he has one of the most brilliant minds of this century; besides being the leader of more than a billion Catholics, he has written thirteen encyclicals, three of which are documents of social reform.

When I was in high school and college, I was a member of a Catholic organization named Accion Catolica de la Juventud Mexicana, or ACJM. ACJM was founded in 1913 to encourage piety, study, and action. Thousands of members gave their lives during the Catholic persecution, the religious war, in Mexico between 1926 and 1929. This persecution was also called the War of the Cristeros, because the fighters often shouted, *"Viva Cristo Rey!"* (Long live Christ the King!) before dying in battle. At ACJM meetings we would review the important social reform encyclicals from the Vatican. Of particular interest were *Rerum Novarum*, by Pope Leo XIII, written in 1891, and *Quadragesimo Anno,* by Pope Pius XI, written in 1931. Of the thirteen encyclicals that Pope John Paul II has written, the three of direct social reform content are: (a) *Laborem Exercens* (1981), (b) *Sollecitudo Rei Socialis* (1987), and (c) *Centesimus Annus* (1991). Because of my background, I consider social reform a vital issue, and I cannot but feel that Pope John Paul II's important documents have not received the attention they deserve.

The audience with His Holiness John Paul II lasted about two hours. At the end of the general audience, those in the prima fila advanced to the front and were able to shake hands with His Holiness. I was the tenth person who climbed the stairs to His Holiness, and when my turn came, the monsignor who was introducing each person leaned toward the Pope and said, *"Lui a scritto un bellisimo libro"* (He has written a beautiful book). I shook hands with His Holiness and gave him the copy of my manuscript, which he received graciously. For me, this was the crowning moment of my research.

Chapter 15

LOOKING
TO THE FUTURE

S CIENCE IS ONE THING, POLITICS ANOTHER. YOU CAN-
not blot out the sunlight by holding up a finger. For me the
Shroud was authentic from the beginning. I knew that an unsuspected
contaminant on the flax fibers was responsible for the wrong radiocarbon dating. It was similar to coating on the Maya artifacts I had
studied. And the radiocarbon test did not seem to me capable of
providing us with unimpeachable information. The date found by the
radiocarbon scientists did not affect my belief in the authenticity of
the Shroud, since I had been able to find out why my Maya artifacts
had been wrongly dated. For me, the Shroud is very clear. The image
on it was created by a natural phenomenon, the presence of bacteria.
And it is these bacteria that made a plastic coating to protect their
work. This seems to me the clearest explanation. There is no doubt
about the presence of the bioplastic coating, no doubt that we have
the empty tubules when the flax is digested. But if anyone wants to
doubt it, even if he is not practicing good science, we will respect
him.

. . .

The bacteria that formed the plastic coat have helped to protect the image and preserve the linen of the Shroud. The Shroud is a naturally plasticized textile. How long these bacteria will be allowed to continue their protective function is a decision that will be made by human beings. My research was stalled by one section of the Catholic authority; that is, the Turin authority. The Pope, in his letter to me, did not ask me to stop my research. I do not intend to appeal to His Holiness directly, because I am pleased with the research as it is now. I just want to continue my research in microbiology, looking for the mechanism used by the bacteria to produce the bioplastic (probably a medium-chain-length polyhydroxyalkanoate) coating. I have the cultures. That work is not being hampered.

So my research will concentrate on the bacteria and the wooden remnants found in the occipital region of the Man on the Shroud. We need to know all about the different bacteria and fungi on the Shroud and determine whether there are other sites of the shoulder or head that may contain more wooden remnants.

The bacteria I have already isolated grow at extreme conditions of pH; some are extreme haloalkaliphilic (bacteria that grow in hyper saline and alkaline environments); others, like the *Leobacillus rubrus*, besides producing the polymer (PHA), a plastic similar to polypropylene, produces an antifungal, which protects the Shroud from fungi. This does not mean that there are no fungi on the Shroud, but they are not in the heavy concentrations found on other ancient textiles. I am interested in knowing what type of molecule this antifungal substance is. One of the bacteria I found on the Shroud, an extreme haloalkaliphilic bacterium that grows on natron, a mixture of sodium carbonate and sodium bicarbonate (in modern household terms, washing soda and baking soda), is what the Egyptians used in the mummification process. When I got the results from the cultures of the bacteria grown in natron, I told Riggi that some bacteria were thriving on natron. In one of his reports he had said that the Shroud had natron remnants, and he was correct. According to the New

Testament, rolls of spices were used in the burial of Jesus of Nazareth, and I think that natron was among them. It was most likely mixed with myrrh. The point is that natron was a substance used not only as a dehydrant, but also as a component of aromatics. Many of the perfumes or aromatics used by the Jews contain natron. This is something that calls for further research, both on the Shroud and on other ancient burial linens.

I also feel that the STURP people made a big mistake in not recognizing what Max Frei accomplished when he took pollen samples from the Shroud back in 1978. His work has been neglected; for me, he ranks with Barbet and Vignon as one of the best scientific researchers of the Shroud. The pollens have been an uncomfortable subject for the scientists, because Max Frei did excellent work, and many people did not want to recognize his contribution. He has been blamed unfairly by people trying to negate his contribution.

My research has confirmed many of Frei's findings. Like Frei, I found pollen, but I also found phytoliths, which do not travel with the wind the way that pollen does, so they might be a major factor in locating the sites where the Shroud may have traveled, an aspect that needs further research.

I am still working with the plastics (reserve polymers) produced by the Shroud's bacteria. There are several types of this PHA, each with different physical characteristics, different resistance to acids, to oxidizers, and to temperature. I believe the composition of the coating on different ancient artifacts will turn out to have slight differences, because the make-up depends on the growing conditions and on the specific strain of the bacteria. Some of these bacteria produce plastic in which the main component is betahydroxybutyric acid; other bacteria have as the main component betahydroxyvaleric acid; others produce mcl-PHA or medium-chain-length PHA with octanoic or decanoic betahydroxyacids. I know from the tests we have done on the cultures from the Shroud that the polyhydroxyalkanoate (PHA) is heat resistant. I have no doubt that this is one of the properties that helped the Shroud survive the fires it has been in. But until I have the exact structure of that PHA, I will not issue scientific reports. I know that the bioplastic is present, and I know that the general name for the polymer is PHA, or polyhydroxyalkanoate. But I want to have the specific structure of the one on the Shroud before I report it. To this end I am awaiting word from Dr. Eggink, of the University of Wageningen in the Netherlands, who is currently analyzing a sample produced by the cultures. It will not be long before we get the results.

My papers have already appeared in three symposium publications, one for the American Society of Human Genetics and two for the American Society for Microbiology. Of these two, one was held in Washington, the other in New Orleans. These were not large papers, just abstracts. With Professor Gove, Professor Mattingly, and Dr. Rosalie David I have also published the findings on Danny the Mummy in the scientific journal *Nuclear Instruments and Methods in Physics Research*. Of course, we could not call him Danny the Mummy in this! Instead, the paper was very properly titled "A Problematic Source of Organic Contamination in Linen." I hope to publish an article in *Science* once the Dutch results are available, but I am in no hurry. With or without peer reviews, I know the bioplastic coating is present on the fibers. Anyone who says that he cannot believe in the coating because it has not been reported in a peer review is not being honest—or is not capable of thinking for himself.

Research on any type of two-thousand-year-old linen would show evidence of PHA, even though the types may differ. Only aseptic conditions would lead to its absence. The PHA of the Shroud is heat resistant and is important because it is biodegradable and therefore may prove of help to humanity. It is important to find the exact structure, because of its many possible applications. Of course the research that most needs to be done is new radiocarbon dating on a sample that is entirely free of contaminants. We know that Cardinal Saldarini still has a portion of the Shroud taken in 1988 during Cardinal Ballestrero's reign. This is the sample that should be used, with the current Cardinal's blessing. If we were given permission, we would repeat the same tests we have already done, under controlled official conditions, but we would use a buffer with no organic compound, like a phosphate. And we would first test our cleaning method on other artifacts, such as pieces from Mummy 1770, before we risked destroying a portion of the Shroud unnecessarily and with no satisfactory outcome.

As currently envisaged, the sample obtained by the digestion of cellulase would first be chemically analyzed to ensure that it is pure glucose, with no contaminant, and to ensure there are no proteins from the bacteria or from the enzyme and no muramic acid from the bacteria. If any of these contaminants showed up in the final powder, we would not proceed to the final stage of radiocarbon dating by the AMS laboratories. But I believe that with all safeguards in place, we have a method of cleaning that will remove the contaminants, the bacteria, the fungi, and the bioplastic coating that so skewed the original radiocarbon dating. And we shall produce a date that will show the Shroud of Turin to be authentic after all.

Finally, and most important, how should we preserve this miraculous cloth? Since the fire on the night of April 11, 1997, which damaged the cathedral and the immediate area where the Shroud was kept, the Shroud itself has been secretly stored elsewhere. It is due, however, to be brought out for public exhibition in the year 2000. I have heard that the Cardinal was offered a plan for the Shroud to be stored and displayed in an oxygen-free environment. In the last exhibition, from April to June 1998, it was in argon. In my opinion, this would be disastrous. This is because one of the bacteria I isolated, *Leobacillus rubrus*, specifically grows in the absence of oxygen. It is a facultative anaerobe that can grow in an inert environment. This type of conservation may destroy the ecological balance, leading to the acceleration of distortion of the image. There might also be some form of destruction I cannot specify at this moment. More studies of the microbiology of the Shroud are needed. Remember, I could study only the trimmings of the samples taken in 1988. It is very dangerous to change the balance that God has provided. When humans intervene, they are in danger of destroying what nature has protected by itself.

We have already seen the color changes that occur when the Shroud is exhibited, under normal conditions, caused by the micro-aerophilic properties of the bacteria. This bacterium is unique. In the Santa Rosa Hospital laboratory that was helping me with the cultures, the technicians jokingly called these bacteria the "divine bugs"; they had never before seen this kind of bacterial activity. If the Shroud is exhibited unprotected, its image will glow even more brightly. In the last two exhibitions, the Shroud was displayed in a box—in 1978, with nitrogen, and in 1998 with argon. This could destroy the balance of the microorganisms on the Shroud. Let us pray that this will not happen, or we shall be sorry for the rest of our lives.

I believe that we are now living in a period of agnosticism and that we want to base every aspect of our lives, including our religion, on scientific proof. This is a moment when the Shroud will help again. In the past, devotion to the Shroud strengthened people spiritually in the midst of plagues and disasters. Today we have a modern plague: the crisis of AIDS, with an estimated forty million victims, sixteen thousand new patients daily. Reverence for the Shroud and belief in God's mercy can help us to face this crisis, and many others as well. So my plea is: Do not let anyone inadvertently destroy the miraculous image that God has provided. Leave the bacteria alone to continue to protect the cloth just as they have done so successfully for the last two thousand years.

Appendix A

ANATOMY, BLOOD, AND DNA ON THE SHROUD

PART 1: ANATOMY OF THE MAN
ON THE SHROUD

The Holy Shroud of Turin is still mysterious, but is certainly not the work of any human hand. This, one can now say, is demonstrated. We said mysterious, because the sacred object still involves many problems, but certainly it is more sacred than perhaps any other: and, as now established in the most positive way, even apart from any idea of faith or Christian piety, it is certainly not a human work.
—POPE PIUS XI, SEPTEMBER 7, 1936. *Osservatore Romano*

WHEN YOU LOOK AT THE FRONTAL IMAGE ON THE Shroud of Turin, you have the impression that you are seeing a man, standing, with his hands crossed over his pubis, the left hand over the right. His mouth is closed, and his long hair, parted on the center, can be seen on both sides of his face as it falls over his shoulders. He appears to have a mustache and a forked beard. The hair is long and comes together to what looks like a "ponytail" ending halfway down his back.[1]

The face of the Man on the Shroud has several swollen areas. A large contusion on his right cheek extends to the cartilage of the nose, which appears fractured and slightly deviated. There is another contusion under the right eye. The cheekbones look bruised and swollen, and a trail of blood flows from each nostril; the left nostril seems swollen and deformed. The blood flows down the left cheek. The swelling of the right cheekbone has partly closed the eye. The short beard contains multiple clots of blood.

SCOURGING

The body, both along the front and the back, contains multiple abrasions, each about three centimeters long. It has been reported that these lesions were made by the *flagrum,* the scourging whip used by the Romans. The man on the Shroud is naked; the lesions on his hips, legs, and buttocks are of the same shape and depth as those on the rest of the body. Opinion varies about the position of Jesus during the scourging. Some believe that he was lying on a short column with his arms on the column; others believe Jesus was bound to a tall vertical beam. Each blow of the flagrum ruptured the skin, causing the body to bleed. It appears that the whip used on Jesus of Nazareth had three thin, stiff ropes, each ending with two small metal balls in the shape of dumbbells. The lesions caused by the scourging are seen on the body as small diagonal slashes. Because the slash angles are in two directions, we believe that two executioners whipped Christ. Each person with a flagrum was probably standing on a different side of Jesus; it has been calculated that they probably stood about a meter away from the victim. The lesions number about 120, and the body of Jesus of Nazareth was covered in blood from his head to his feet.

CROWN OF THORNS

The Man on the Shroud wore a crown made of thorns. Dr. Judica-Cordiglia, a forensic doctor in Milan, has graphically described the wounds inflicted by this particular cruelty:

> *Singular traces of drops of blood can be seen all around the perimeter of the head at the level where the forehead and temples are located. These bleeding points are the result of the lesions on the scalp. Considering their distribution, in the form of an aureola, we can deduce that they were caused by objects that were sharp, prickly, and nailed, in the shape of a crown or hood, and rubbed over the head.*[2]

Dr. Rodante, describing the lesions in detail, indicated that each thorn must have damaged a site on the scalp by perforating a blood vessel. It is even possible that one blood vessel was damaged by two thorns at the same time.[3]

On the forehead and on both temporal areas there are at least thirteen traces of perforations by a sharp and pointed object. The coagulated blood on the occipital region (back of the head) came together. It is not possible to distinguish each trail of blood hidden in the thick hair. Nevertheless, by extrapolating from the number of visible perforations and their consistent spacing on the front of the forehead, we can postulate that approximately twenty thorns pierced the occipital region. On the frontal area, a small blood stream coagulated, forming a clot shaped like the Greek letter epsilon or (a reversed figure 3). This has been called "the seal of authenticity of the Shroud."

Another important frontal bleeding was described by Dr. Giuseppe Casselli:

> *While analyzing these lesions we can see over the right temple, at the base of the hair, a small sharp wound from which*

flow two small streams of blood. One is angled and descends the length of the hair as far as the shoulder. The other flows vertically down the forehead to the ridge of the brow. The thorn apparently injured the frontal branch of the temporal artery.

Dr. Caselli also commented on the hemorrhage at the central of the forehead:

Looking toward the left of the center of the forehead, we can see a hemorrhage, in the shape of an epsilon . . . whose blood is of a uniform shade, opaque, and very dark. It has the characteristics of venous blood, which differentiate it from the blood on the right temple described earlier. Here, the thorn has clearly wounded the frontal vein, known by the anatomists as the prepared vein. It is sometimes single but is generally double, as it is in this case. The odd shape—the epsilon or reversed 3—may have been brought about by the wrinkling of the frontal muscle in a spasm of pain.[4]

The nape of the neck presents about twelve wounds, with signs of bleeding on both sides.

THE ROAD TO CALVARY

After being scourged and crowned with thorns, Jesus was to be put to death by crucifixion. The accused carried the cross, on his shoulders, from the prison up to the place of execution. As Jesus and the other two prisoners walked, they were surrounded by four soldiers, a *tetradion*, who were commanded by a centurion. The cross used by the Romans was made up of two parts: the vertical element, which usually was fixed in place at the site of the executions, was the *stipes,* and the horizontal beam, which the accused carried on his shoulders, was the *patibulum.*

The image on the Shroud of the back of the body shows one bruise at the level of the right scapular (shoulder blade), extending to the top of the shoulder. Another bruise, on the left scapular region, shows even more damage and signs of a wound. On the painful way to Calvary, or Golgotha—to the northwest and outside the city of Jerusalem—Jesus suffered three falls that caused severe wounds to his knees and face. Dr. Cordiglia described them:

> *The knees are of particular interest. The right knee is not only more damaged but has several scrapes of different sizes and shapes. Somewhat above and toward the exterior are two round open sores, one above the other, each with a diameter of about 2 centimeters.*[5]

Dr. Cordiglia added:

> *The left knee, also bruised and marked with scrapes of different sizes and shapes, is not as badly injured as the right knee. The wounds on this knee, because of their direction and location, give us some indication of where the falls took place. It was an uneven terrain covered with rocks of different sizes.*

Since Jesus had his arms tied to the horizontal beam, the patibulum, he must have seriously wounded his face on the rocks with each fall, thereby producing large lesions. The peeling of the skin on his feet and the mud on the feet indicate that he walked barefoot to his execution site. After Jesus of Nazareth had his robe taken from him, he was placed on the floor above the patibulum, and his wrists—not his hands—were nailed to the beam. The two executioners, after having nailed both wrists to the patibulum, probably forced Jesus to stand, and they then must have raised the beam and inserted it into the stipes in such a way that the body hung by the arms. It has been calculated that the weight of the body pulling on the arms put them at an angle of 65 degrees. The executioners then nailed his feet to the vertical beam. On the back image of the Shroud can be seen the complete print of the right foot and the heel and the central part of the left foot. Dr. Barbet believes that only one nail was used for both feet, but Dr. Cordiglia believes that two nails were used, one for the right foot and another for the left.[6]

THE DEATH OF JESUS OF NAZARETH

A jar full of vinegar stood there, so putting a sponge soaked in the vinegar on a hyssop stick they held it up to his mouth. After Jesus had taken the vinegar he said, 'It is accomplished'; and bowing his head, he gave up his spirit.

—JOHN 19:29–30

It has been said that the death of Jesus of Nazareth took place on Friday, April 7, 30 (Nisan 14 on the Hebrew calendar).[7] The cause of death was the accumulation of many pathological factors, not a single wound. The first of these was the mental agony Jesus suffered at the Mount of Olives in the Garden of Gethsemane. It was the first day of Passover, when unleavened bread was eaten. During his prayers, he underwent severe mental stress, knowing what the immediate future held.

In his anguish he prayed even more earnestly and his sweat fell to the ground like great drops of blood.

—LUKE 22:44

Blood sweat (hematidrosis) has been reported by several medical doctors in cases of severe mental anguish. We have the observations of Dr. Klauder, a dermatologist in Philadelphia, on the case of Teresa Newman. Dr. Klauder examined Teresa Newman during one of these blood-sweat episodes.[8] Other cases of hematidrosis have been reported by Dr. Schindler[9] and Dr. Jacobi.[10] On November 6, 1926, Dr. Seidl observed Teresa Newman during a state of ecstasy. He found that she was bleeding from three different places on the scalp.

Another cause of the loss of blood was the scourging Jesus endured. It decreased the amount of liquid in the intravascular compartment by transferring fluids to the intersticial space. The transfer resulted from the formation of ecchymosis and hematomas in the damaged skin areas.

Edwards et al. published a paper in the *Journal of the American Medical Association* entitled "On the Physical Death of Jesus Christ." The authors reported: "The severe scourging, with its intense pain and appreciable blood loss, most probably left Jesus in a preshock state . . . Therefore, even before the actual crucifixion, Jesus' physical condition was at least serious and possibly critical."[11]

Jesus' carrying the patibulum, which had a calculated weight of 75 to 125 pounds,[12] to Golgotha, required strenuous effort. He did not have the strength and had to be helped. Simon of Cyrene carried the patibulum the remainder of the distance. This expenditure of energy contributed to the preshock state.[13]

According to some historians, the Persians were the first to execute by crucifixion. Others believe the Phoenicians were the first. In any case, the practice spread to Egypt and Carthage, and the Romans learned of it from the Carthaginians. It is believed that the cross used in the crucifixion of Jesus of Nazareth was the *crux commisa,* also known as the Tau cross, that is, shaped like the Greek letter *tau.* This was the cross used by the Romans in Palestine in the first century.

The nails in the wrists damaged the median nerve so that each movement of the body produced excruciating pain in both arms and made the hands clench.[14] The crucifixion also caused severe respiratory impairment, especially during exhalation. The weight of the body on the stretched arms fixed the intercostal muscles during inhalation, making exhalation the more painful. The victim resorted to the diaphragm for weak abdominal respirations, and those pushed on the nail in the feet. Because respiration was not complete, carbon dioxide was retained by the lungs, causing respiratory acidosis.

When Jesus was on the cross, he lifted himself by pushing on his feet to aid his breathing, his body scraped on the wood, opening some of the lesions. Every time he pushed on the nail in his feet, he suffered further pain. When his hands moved under pressure, the nail produced intolerable pain in the median nerve. This exacerbated the hypovolemia and the respiratory acidosis, triggering a state of shock.

It is believed that Jesus was on the cross for three to six hours. One explanation of his apparently sudden death is that Jesus suffered a myocardial infarction with rupture of the left ventricle. I do not believe this is what happened. According to Saint John, blood and water drained from the chest of Jesus when it was pierced by the spear of the centurion. After a rupture, the blood from the ventricular cavity is mixed together with the pericardial fluid. It does not appear first as blood and then as water; death is instantaneous.

In "Death by Crucifixion," a 1963 paper by DePasquale and Burch, the authors state that death was by suffocation. After Jesus was exhausted by the attempts to breathe, lifting his body and pushing at the nail in his feet, he had respiratory arrest and lapsed into unconsciousness and death.[15]

In 1964, Tenney wrote his ideas in *The American Heart Journal* (which had published the report by DePasquale and Burch). His paper, "On Death by Crucifixion," covers his complete disagreement with DePasquale and Burch. He wrote:

In brief, the new proposition that the mechanism of death was by suffocation, consequent to fixation of the respiratory bellows and exhaustion of the muscles of respiration, does not seem likely to me . . . Scourging produced physical exhaustion and shock, carrying the cross further weakened the victim, and then hanging on the cross led to hypotension, circulatory collapse, and death.[16]

The cause of death of Jesus cannot be scientifically proved. In the study of the Shroud of Turin, there are observations that can support more than one hypothesis. It is probable that the death of Jesus of Nazareth on the cross had a multifactorial cause. Hypovolemic shock, orthostatic hypotension, and asphyxia were all factors that precipitated the death. The spear wound at the right side of Jesus' chest was inflicted after the death. The drainage of blood and water from the chest wound indicated that there was no rupture of the heart ventricle after a production of a myocardial infarction, as some scientists have suggested. Rather, it shows that the heart was lacerated with the spear. After many years of work in pediatrics and cardiology, I can report the catastrophic consequences of heart punctures and leaking of blood through loose sutures in the heart. The idea that Jesus did not die on the cross, as some authors have claimed, is absurd and unscientific.

Dr. Hynek comments about the agony in Jesus:

The death on the cross was really the most atrocious. The strength of the accused was consumed slowly and it provoked terrible cramps . . . that with all consciousness would extend to his diaphragm muscle that separates his chest from his abdomen, and to all the muscles in his thorax.[17]

The Romans did not break Jesus' legs, as was usually done, due to his premature death, but they did pierce his right side, as I have described. The large bloodstain in the right side of the chest continuing to the small of the back is the drainage of blood through this wound as the corpse was moved to the tomb or after it was deposited in the tomb.

THE OFFICIAL REPORT
BY A FORENSIC PATHOLOGIST

Dr. Robert Bucklin, deputy coroner and forensic pathologist at the Los Angeles County Hospital, gives his expert reading of the negatives of the Man on the Shroud. (The words were slightly changed by Dr. J. H. Heller.)[18]

Irrespective of how the images were made, there is adequate information here to state that they are anatomically correct. There is no problem in diagnosing what happened to this individual. The pathology and physiology are unquestionable and represent medical knowledge unknown 150 years ago. This is a 5-foot, 11-inch male Caucasian weighing about 178 pounds. The lesions are as follows: beginning at the head, there are blood flows from numerous puncture wounds on the top and back of the scalp and forehead. The man has been beaten about the face, there is a swelling over one cheek, and he undoubtedly has a black eye. His nose tip is abraded, as would occur from a fall, and it appears that the nasal cartilage may have separated from the bone. There is a wound in the left wrist, the right one being covered by the left hand. This is the typical lesion of a crucifixion. The classical artistic and legendary portrayal of a crucifixion with nails through the palms of the hands is spurious: the structures in the hand are too fragile to hold the live weight of a man, particularly of this size. Had a man been crucified with nails in the palms, they would have torn through the bones, muscles, and ligaments, and the victim would have fallen off the cross.

There is a stream of blood down both arms. Here and there, there are blood drips at an angle from the main blood flow in response to gravity. These angles represent the only ones that can occur from the only two positions which can be taken by a body during crucifixion.

On the back and on the front there are lesions which appear to be scourge marks. Historians have indicated that Romans used a whip called a flagrum. This whip had two or three thongs, and at their ends there were pieces of metal or bone which look like small dumbbells. These were designed to gouge out flesh. The thongs and metal end-pieces from a Roman flagrum fit precisely into the anterior and posterior scourge lesions on the body. The victim was whipped from both sides by two men, one of whom was taller than the other, as demonstrated by the angle of the thongs.

There is a swelling of both shoulders, with abrasions indicating that something heavy and rough had been carried across the man's shoulders within hours of death. On the right flank, a long, narrow blade of some type entered in an upward direction, pierced the diaphragm, penetrated into the thoracic cavity through the lung into the heart. This was a post-mortem event, because separate components of red cells and clear serum drained from the lesion. Later, after the corpse was laid out horizontally and face up on the cloth, blood dribbled out of the side wound and puddled along the small of the back. There is no evidence of either

leg being fractured. There is an abrasion of one knee, com-
mensurate with a fall (as is the abraded nose tip); and, fi-
nally, a spike had been driven through both feet, and blood
had leaked from both wounds onto the cloth. The evidence
of a scourged man who was crucified and died from the
cardiopulmonary failure typical of crucifixion is clear-cut.

Appendix A

ANATOMY, BLOOD, AND DNA ON THE SHROUD

PART 2: HUMAN BLOOD
ON THE SHROUD

THIRTY YEARS AGO, ON JUNE 16 AND 17, 1969, THERE was a meeting of experts, organized by Cardinal Michele Pellegrino. The purpose was to study the Shroud of Turin. Three scientists—Giorgio Frache, Eugenia Maria Rizatti, and Emilio Mari— who concentrated on the bloodstains, concluded that the stains on the Shroud were not blood. In 1978 new samples were lifted from the Shroud's blood marks by Dr. Pierre Luigi Baima-Bollone, from Italy, and Dr. Raymond Rogers, from the American group STURP, using adhesive tapes. Dr. Rogers gave some of these tapes to Dr. Walter McCrone and to the team formed by Dr. John H. Heller and Dr. Alan Adler from Connecticut.

The conclusions of each group were different. In Italy, Dr. Baima Bollone reported human blood of type AB. In America, Dr. McCrone reported that the stains on the Shroud were not blood; they were the earth pigment red ochre and vermillion. Dr. McCrone concluded that the stains on the cloth were pigments deposited by an artist. In opposition to this, Dr. Adler and Dr. Heller concluded that the stains were true blood.

I have studied several blood samples from the occipital region on the Shroud's dorsal image. These samples were taken by Riggi di Numana on April 21, 1988, the same day that samples were obtained for radiocarbon tests. Thanks to the courtesy of Dr. Adler, I have also studied a sample from the area of the left hand of the frontal image, obtained from the tapes taken by Dr. Rogers in 1978.

I used the following techniques:

1. Direct observation with the optical microscope
2. Histochemical techniques
   a. Mallory's Prussian blue reaction
   b. Wright's stain
3. Immunohisto-chemical techniques
   a. Antibody anti-antigen B and anti-antigen H
   b. Antibody anti-human adult hemoglobin

Direct analysis with the optical microscope, and with phase-contrast microscope, of the hand blood sample showed that the material was organic (cellular), not crystalline (pigments), as had been previously reported by some.

The blood smears had been replaced almost completely (95 percent) by fungi and bacteria. By using oil immersion (1000X), I found with the optical microscope that the fungi were Ascomycetes, with bitunicate and pseudoparaphysis in the fungi locule.

A blood smear from the occipital area of the dorsal image was stained with Wright's technique for blood. The smear had been almost completely replaced by fungi, but some cell-like structures were seen. A Mallory's Prussian blue reaction, done to stain the iron of the blood remnant, showed that only a small area of the smear held iron.

Several immunohisto-chemical tests, using antibodies anti-antigen B and anti-antigen H (group O), were used. Again, only a small area of the remnant stained positive for antigen B. A reaction obtained by using an antibody against adult hemoglobin showed results similar to the previous one. Only a small area of the sample reacted positive, proving again that more than 95 percent of the blood remnants have been replaced by bacteria and fungi.

Dr. W. McCrone reported his initial research on the tapes taken by Dr. Rogers from the Shroud in 1978 during the STURP studies. In *The Microscope Journal,* volume 28[1, 2] and volume 29[3] he said there was no blood on the Shroud. In 1990 he published a paper, in the *Accounts of Chemical Research,*[4] again stating that no blood was present on the Shroud.

The photographs of the Shroud fibers published by Dr. McCrone in *The Microscope Journal* in 1981 are excellent. His Figures 1 and 3 look similar to my findings of the bioplastic coating on the Shroud fibers. He was correct in not accepting the idea that oxidative dehydration of the cellulose was the reason for the "image formation." The presence of iron oxide (hematite) in the fibers' organic deposits is explained by the deposits of the chemolithotrophic bacteria. There are five types of chemolithotrophs: (a) hydrogen bacteria; (b) sulfur bacteria; (c) iron or manganese bacteria; (d) ammonia oxidizers; and (e) nitrite oxidizers.[5] The bacteria that oxidize iron obtain part of their energy by the removal of one electron from the ferrous ion, with the production of a ferric ion, which precipitates in the form of hematite.

The presence of hematite on the Shroud was documented not only in the blood areas, but also in the image areas and in the nonimage areas. In the bacteria chemolithotrophs, the final receptor of the electrons removed from the iron ions is oxygen, which means that it is an aerobic process. The process in the anaerobic phototrophs, in which there is no release of electrons, and protons are bound to oxygen and do not form water, is known as *cyclic photophosphorylation.* In this process the *bacteriochlorophylls* serve as both the electron donors and the electron receptors.

As we have seen, 95 percent of the blood areas on the Shroud have been taken over by fungi and bacteria, and the small amount of blood still present continues to diminish with time. In the near future there will be no more blood on the Shroud. Some blood smears have been completely replaced already. We can state that after our isolation of the human DNA from the Shroud with the cloning of the three gene segments, there is no doubt of the presence of human blood from a male on the Shroud.

Ancient blood deposited on the Itzamna Tun.

From left to right: *M. Gabriel Vial, Franco A. Testore, Giovanni Riggi di Numana. Turin, Italy, April 21, 1988.*

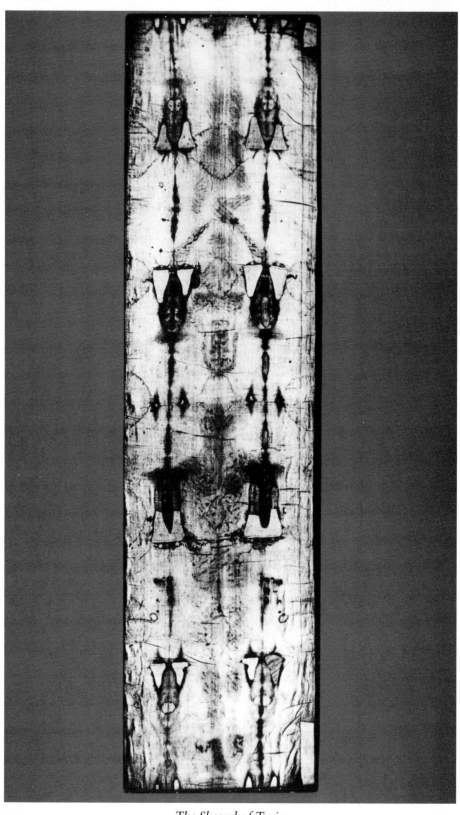

The Shroud of Turin
(courtesy Don Bosco Filmstrips)

Father Faustino Cervantes Ibarrola
(right) and Professor Riggi.

Professor Riggi opening the petri
dish with the Shroud samples,
which is stamped with Riggi and
Gonella's seal.

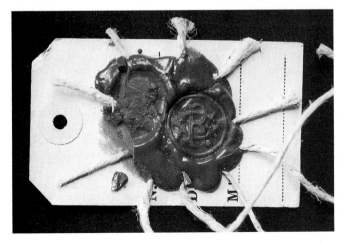

Close-up of Giovanni
Riggi and Luigi
Gonella's seal stamped
in red wax.

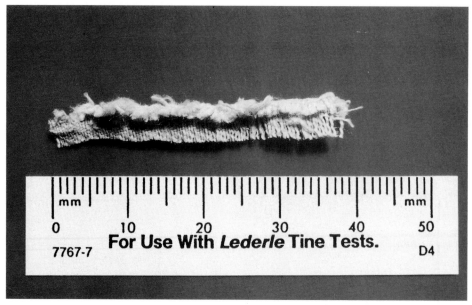

Shroud Sample A. Trimmed sample originally taken for 1988 radiocarbon dating.

Father Cervantes and the author in front of the silver reliquary containing the Shroud at St. John the Baptist Cathedral in Turin.

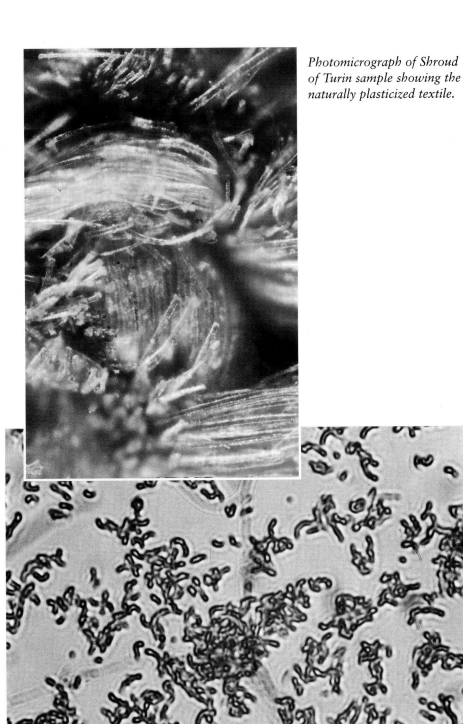

Photomicrograph of Shroud of Turin sample showing the naturally plasticized textile.

Leobacillus rubrus *(400X) with Gram stain.*

Scanning electron microscopy photomicrograph of Shroud's non-image fibers, showing the acrylico-polymer coating.

Photomicrograph of a thread from the Shroud that had an increase in bioplastic coating after being in a culture of dextrose for four weeks.

Dr. Harry E. Gove and the author outside St. Patrick's Cathedral in New York City.

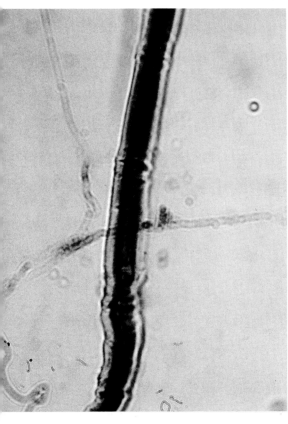
Photomicrograph of Shroud of Turin fiber. Flax fiber stained in purple with covering of bioplastic coating.

Danny the ibis mummy.

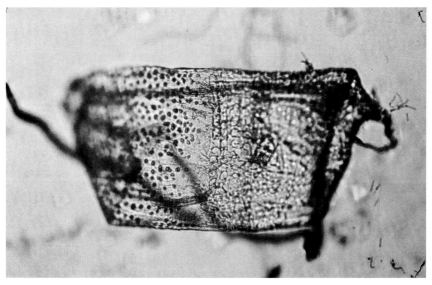

Oak wood vessel found in occipital region dorsal image of the Shroud.

ANATOMY, BLOOD, AND DNA ON THE SHROUD

Part 3: Human DNA on the Shroud. The DNA of God?

"The Father and I are one."

—JOHN 10:30

L IFE IS TRANSFERRED FROM ONE LIVING ORGANISM, OR species, to another by DNA. If there was no DNA, reproduction would not be possible. In a eukaryote, a single- or multicelled organism containing a nucleus, the DNA is in long threads of chromosomes. The chromosomes are formed by the coded repetition of four basic units known as nucleotides. Each nucleotide molecule has three components, a base, a sugar, and a molecule of phosphoric acid. There are four bases for the nucleotides in DNA: adenine (A), cytosine (C), guanine (G), and thymine (T). The sugar in the four nucleotides is deoxyribose.

The structure of the nucleotides is made up of two sets of pairs.

Guanine is paired with cytosine; adenine is paired with thymine. These complementary pairs, known as *base pairs,* make up the two threads that form each chromosome (the double helix). The sequence in which the four nucleotides—A, C, G, and T—are arranged in the threads (the chromosomes) determines the sequence of the working molecules (proteins).

The position of three nucleotides—the *codon*—in the large DNA molecule determines the position of an amino acid, one of the building blocks of the proteins. The number of base pairs in the human genome is three billion.[1] All three billion base pairs are assembled in forty-six chromosomes. Each chromosome has two intertwined threads, the *chromatids.* Each chromatid has a single, genetically specific DNA molecule and also has many proteins that help to translate the code to the next molecule in the genetic code, the *transfer RNA.*

The DNA molecules transfer their genetic information to the ribosomes in the cell cytoplasm; they are the sites of the synthesis, the production, of the proteins through molecules of RNA. (In RNA, the sugar deoxyribose of the DNA is replaced by ribose.) Each of the RNA molecules that transfer the genetic code from the chromosomes to the ribosomes is a *messenger RNA (mRNA).*

HUMAN CHROMOSOMES

The human species has forty-six chromosomes (twenty-two pairs of autosomes and two sexual chromosomes, XX in females and XY in males). They are usually denoted as 46:XY in the normal male and as 46:XX in the normal female. The chromosomes are studied in the human cells (generally leukocytes or cells from the mucosa of the mouth) during the phase known as *metaphase.* The chromosomes are organized according to size, from the longest to the shortest, with the shorter arm of each chromosome pointing upward, a display known as a *karyotype.*

The normal human embryo needs the two sexual chromosomes for development. If one of the sexual chromosomes is missing or an extra one is added, the fetus will have severe anomalies. If there is only one sexual chromosome and it is the X chromosome (45:XO), the resulting anomaly is Turner's syndrome. If two X chromosomes combine with a Y chromosome (47:XXY), the result is Klinefelter's syndrome. If two X chromosomes combine with another X chromosome, forming the triple X syndrome (47:XXX), the anomaly is a phenotypical female. The chromosome formula (45:YO) is not viable; the product dies before development.

SEX IDENTIFICATION BY PCR

To study the sex of blood or cells, you may use the *testis-determining factor* (TDF), which is present only in males, or you may use the *amelogenin genes,* present in both sexes. The female gene is longer than the male gene, so we decided to use the amelogenin-X gene (AMG) and the amelogenin-like Y gene (AMGL). The sequence in the genes AMG and AMGL diverged about 25 million years ago.[2]

A paper published in *The American Journal of Medical Genetics,* by Nakahori et al., reported the use of the two amelogenin genes for sex identification, according to the polymerase chain reaction (PCR). The AMG and AMGL genes produce the proteins that are present in tooth enamel. The AMG is 177 base pairs longer than the AMGL.

The two primers used for the PCR tests of these two genes are:

AMXY-1F (5′-CTGATGGTTGGCCTCAAGCCTGTG-3′)
AMXY-2R (5′-TAAAGAGATTCATTAACTTGALTG-3′)

The X fragment and the Y fragment have different lengths. The X-band is longer (177 bp) than the Y-band, so its speed is different; the Y band travels faster than the X band. The male has two different bands; the female has a single, thicker band. On the first day of January of each year, the church celebrates the feast of the circumcision of the Lord. If this was accomplished, the chromosome formula of Jesus of Nazareth, a normal baby boy, had to be 46:XY.

PCR TESTS IN THE BLOOD REMNANTS OF THE SHROUD

Blood remnants from the Shroud, from the areas of the left hand (taken by the STURP group in 1978) and from the occipital region (taken by Riggi on April 21, 1988), were tested with PCR for the presence of three gene segments: (a) betaglobin gene, (b) amelogenin-X gene, and (c) amelogenin-Y gene. The testing was done at the PCR laboratory of the Department of Microbiology at the University of Texas Health Science Center in San Antonio, headed by Dr. Victor Tryon. All three segments of the human genes tested were positive, indicating that the blood of the Man on the Shroud came from a human male. The betaglobin gene from chromosome-11 was the first segment of DNA that was studied and cloned. It is the easiest gene to study, and the results were excellent: 268 base pairs (nucleotides) were cloned. The control used in this cloning was HUMHBB221.

BETAGLOBIN GENE SEGMENT FROM BLOOD ON THE SHROUD: THE DNA OF GOD?

Cloned from Shroud occipital area blood glob:

Con   TCCTAAGCCA GTGCCAGAAG AGCCAAGGAC AGGTACGGCT

GTCATCACTT

1450

Shr   GAAG

AGCCAAGGAC AGGT*NCCAAT* GTCATCACTT   34

TCCTAAGCCA GTGCCA (PRIMER)

Con   AGACCTCACC CTGTGGAGCC ACACCCTAGG GTTGGCCAAT

CTACTCCCAG

1500

Shr   AGACCTCACC CTGTGGAGCC ACACCCTAGG GTTGGCCAAT

CTACTCCCAG

84

Con   GAGCAGGGAG GGCAGGAGCC AGGGCTGGGC ATAAAAGTCA

GGCAGAGCC

1550

Shr   GAGCAGGGAG GGCAGGAGCC AGGGCTGGGC ATAAAAGTCA

GGCAGAGCC

134

Con   ATCTATTGCT TACATTTGCT TCTGACACAA CTGTGTTCAC

TAGCAACCTC

1600

Shr   ATCTATTGCT TACATTTGCT TCTGACACAA CTGTGTTCAC

TAGCAACCTC   184

Con   AAACAGACAC CATGGTGCAC CTGACTCCTG AGGAGAAGTC

TGCCGTTACT

1650

Shr   AAACAGACAC CATGGTGCAC CTGACTCCTG AGGAGAAGTC

TGCCGTTACT

234

Con   GCCCTGTGGG GCAAGGTGAA CGTGGATGAA GTTGGTGGTG

AGGCCCTGGG

1700

Shr   GCCCTGTGGG GCAAGGTGAA CGTGGATGAA GTTG

268

(primer) GTGGTG AGGCCCTGGG

A NATURALLY
PLASTICIZED
TEXTILE

PART 1: THE MICROBIOLOGY
OF THE SHROUD

O N JANUARY 26 AND 27, 1996, THE FIRST INTERNA-
tional Symposium on Archaeomicrobiology was held at
the University of Texas Health Science Center at San Antonio.
Archaeomicrobiology is the study of the ecology, taxonomy, and secondary metabolites produced by microorganisms that have colonized
on the surface of ancient artifacts over the course of time.

Carl R. Woese divided the universal phylogenetic tree into three
domains, the *archaea,* the *bacteria,* and the *eukarya.*[1] All these microorganisms may produce on ancient stable surfaces coatings of diverse
nature, which have been given different names: (a) biogenic varnish,
(b) cataract crust, (c) desert crust, (d) desert lacquer, (e) desert patina,
(f) desert rind, (g) desert varnish, (h) mountain varnish, (i) protective
coatings, (j) rock varnish, and (k) weathering crust.

HISTORY

The first natural coatings described were the dark deposits found on desert rocks. They were first described by Alexander Humbolt in 1793,[2] by Charles Darwin in 1832,[3] and have been studied extensively. Many of the studies were carried out during the first half of the twentieth century.

In 1980 Ronald I. Dorn first used the name *rock varnish* for these natural deposits, and described some microorganisms associated with it.[4] In 1982, Staley et al. described the presence of microcolonial fungi on desert rocks,[5] and in 1983 Taylor-George et al. described the association of bacteria and dematiaceous hyphomycetes in the formation of desert varnish.[6]

In April 1993, at the fifty-eighth Meeting of the Society for American Archaeology, in St. Louis, Missouri, I presented a paper entitled: "Biogenic Varnish on Ancient Pottery and Stone Artifacts." In it, I discussed the natural plastic deposits produced by bacteria on ancient artifacts.[7]

BACTERIAL TAXONOMY

All living organisms are divided into two groups: the *prokaryotes* have a primitive nucleus with no nuclear membranes; the *eukaryotes* have all their genetic information in threads called chromosomes, which are inside a membrane-bound nucleus. To study living organisms systematically, we must classify them. And this classification discipline is called *taxonomy*.

Bacterial taxonomy is the study of the classification, nomenclature, and identification of bacteria, which are the oldest of the living creatures. There are reports of bacteria that are 3.5 billion years old.[8] All the bacteria (prokaryotes) belong to the Kingdom *Prokaryotae* and, according to the Carl Woese classification, are in the Domain *Bacteria.*

The bacteria and the eukaryotes use proteins, the most important molecules in living cells, to control functions like metabolism, growth, and the reproduction of the cells. Proteins are responsible for the metabolism that produces the molecules used as building blocks for the cells. The active protein molecules are the enzymes, formed at the ribosomes in the cells cytoplasm. The amino acid sequence in the enzymes (proteins) is stored in the ribosome nucleic acids (rRNA), which receive the coding for the production of the proteins from the genetic information sent by the DNA through the messenger ribonucleic acid (mRNA) and the aminoacyl transfer ribonucleic acid (tRNA). The DNA molecule that transmits the genetic information has two strands, like two twisted strings of yarn. One of the strings is the coding DNA strand; the other is the template DNA strand.

The ribosomes, or protein factories, are in the cell cytoplasm. The bacteria (prokaryotic) ribosomes are different from the fungi (eukaryotic) ribosomes; they each have a weight of 70S (S refers to a rate of sedimentation of the particles, which is related to their density and is measured on the Svedberg system). The ribosomes of the eukaryotes have a weight of 80S. Each bacterium has between 10,000 and 20,000 ribosomes.[9]

The ribosomes of the prokaryotes (the bacteria with a weight of 70S each) consist of two subparticles of different weights, a 30S subparticle and a 50S subparticle. The small ribosomal subparticle (30S) is composed of a 16S RNA molecule and 21 protein molecules. The large ribosomal subparticle (50S) is composed of a 5S RNA element, a 23S RNA element, and 32 proteins. The three different ribosomal types of RNAs in the prokaryotes are formed by a different number of nucleotides: the 5S rRNA by 120 nucleotides; the 16S rRNA by 1500 nucleotides; and the 23S rRNA by about 3000 nucleotides. The sedimentation rates, or S values, used as measurement units are not directly related to the number of nucleotides. (For example, a 16S molecule is 1500 nucleotides long, but a molecule of 3000 nucleotides is not twice the S unit, but only 23S.)

The process of protein synthesis in the cells is as ancient as the origin of life; it has been transmitted as genetic information (hereditary information). The nucleotide sequence of the ribosomal ribonucleic acids (rRNA) have changed slowly, with the evolution of the different species. Each species has a different sequence of the nucleotides, though there is some similarity among the groups. Each can be studied as a particular fingerprint of a living species, the process of modern taxonomy.

BACTERIAL METABOLISM

In spite of the small size of a bacterium, it is capable of a diversity of metabolic reactions. The volume of the bacterium is a few cubic micrometers, and the surface-to-volume ratio is the greatest found in any living organism. Bacteria are classified into three large groups, according to the way they obtain their nutrients (carbon): the *Heterotrophs,* whose carbon comes from other organic material; the *Autotrophs,* whose source is the carbon dioxide in the air; and *Mixotrophs,* which grow in both conditions. The energy used by bacteria is also obtained by one of three different mechanisms: (a) the reducing power of organic substances (organotrophs), (b) the oxidation of ferrous ions or manganese ions, and (c) radiant energy, like sunlight (phototrophs). In all three mechanisms, the main mode of generating energy is by the transport of electrons. Autotrophs have four ways to capture carbon dioxide from the air: (a) the Calvin cycle, (b) the reductive TCA cycle, (c) the acetyl-CoA pathway, and (d) the glycine synthetase pathway. Autotrophs require only carbon dioxide, nitrogen gas, a few minerals, and an energy source—sunlight or reduced iron or manganese—to grow. Some heterotrophs grow better at a high concentration of carbon dioxide and low concentration of oxygen; they are known as *Microaerophilic*.

For several years I did research on bacteria that grow in alkaline environments and was fortunate to discover four new genera and twenty new species of alkaliphilic and alkali-tolerant bacteria. My research on the microbiology of these alkaline environments (Mexico, Egypt, Eritrea, and Turkey) helped me to understand the behavior of some of the extreme alkaliphilic bacteria found on the Shroud. I also discovered on the Shroud the other extreme, in a group that belongs to the *Proteobacteria*, which are capable of producing acetic acid (vinegar).

ARTIFACT ANALYSES

The surfaces of ancient artifacts have deposits of different microorganisms that may be photosynthetic, iron and manganese oxidizers, and capable of fixing carbon dioxide and nitrogen. These bacteria deposit iron oxide (hematite), manganese oxide, or bioplastic (PHA) on the surface of the artifacts. The study of the metabolic functions of these and other bacteria and fungi may produce information about the artifact's origin, its age, and the environmental conditions it was subjected to.

After my research on Maya jades, I decided to study the bacterial deposits on the Shroud of Turin. To examine these surface deposits I used the following analytical methods:

1. back-scattered electron microscopy (BEM)
2. bacteria and fungi culture media
3. Energy-dispersive spectrometry (EDS)
4. Fourier-transform infrared spectrometry (FT-IR)

5. gas chromatography/mass spectrometry (GC/MS)
6. histological techniques
7. immunohisto-chemical techniques
8. optical microscopy
   a. transmitted
   b. reflected
   c. phase-contrast
   d. polarized with crossed polars
   e. chlorophyll filter
   f. ultraviolet light
9. scanning electron microscopy (SEM)
10. solid probe/mass spectrometry (SP/MS)
11. ultraviolet light (254 and 366 nm)
12. wavelength dispersive spectroscopy (WDS)
13. wet chemistry

Optical microscopy was the first technique used in the analyses of the Shroud's fibers. A yellowish bioplastic coating was found on the surface of the flax fibers, with millions of bacteria and dark brown fungi (dematiaceous hyphomycetes and ascomycetes). With the optical microscope at high magnification, the textile fibers were seen covered with a fishnet pattern formed by filamentous bacteria. Some of the nonimage textile fibers at the thread's crests had pink-pigmented parallel areas deposited by the bacteria.

Several histological sections, using the paraffin method, were done on a segment of a thread from the Shroud. The paraffin sections were stained with the following techniques: (a) acid fast; (b) amido black; (c) Best's carmine; (d) Giemsa; (e) Gimesa's modified; (f) Gram's stain; (g) hematoxylin and eosin; (h) methenamine silver; (i) Papanicolau; (j) periodic acid Schiff's; and (k) toluidine blue.

A thread's thin section, stained with Schiff's reagent, showed the dematiaceous hyphomycetes (black fungi that produce filaments) on the fibers stained in a dark magenta color. With this technique the fibers showed pleochroism in sky blue and magenta. Many bacteria stained in red were seen inside the fiber lumen.

I divided the microbiology study into three sections: (a) acari; (b) bacteria, and (c) fungi.

ACARI

The acari found on the tapes taken from the Shroud were 1.5×2.75 mm.

BACTERIA

Some of the bacteria are still under study. Of the three types that have been isolated, two have been classified: (a) a gram-negative bacillus *(Leobacillus rubrus),* which produces acetic acid, an antifungal, a pink pigment, and plastic (reserve polymer). It has a wide pH range of growth (4.5–10); (b) a gram-positive coccus that belongs to the *Micrococcus luteus* group; and (c) an extreme haloalkaliphilic gram positive–gram variable coccus that grows singly, in pairs, or as filaments in media. It grows in natron (sodium carbonate) and it has an alkaline pH range of growth from 10 to 13. These are still under study.

The culture media used to test the above bacteria were:

1. brain heart infusion agar
2. charcoal yeast extract agar
3. Krumbein K-2 agar
4. noble agar (mineral agar)
5. Sabouraud dextrose agar
6. Tindall's agar
7. Todd-Hewitt agar
8. tryptic soy agar (TSA)
9. tryptic soy broth (TSB)
10. TSA with blood

11. TSA with 5% sodium carbonate

12. TSA with 10% sodium carbonate

The bacteria on the different culture media were grown in (a) room air (b) in anaerobic conditions, and (c) in microaerophilic conditions using 10 percent carbon dioxide. The gases in unpolluted air at sea level are: (a) nitrogen (78.09 percent), (b) oxygen (20.94 percent), (c) rare gases (0.932 percent), and (d) carbon dioxide (0.0345 percent).

Leobacillus rubrus

The gram-negative bacilli (GNBs) isolated from the Shroud have a variable size of 2 to 4 micrometers in length and 1 to 1.5 micrometers in diameter. They occur singly, in pairs, or as filaments. Under certain growth conditions, they produce cystlike structures. Most of the time they stain gram negative, but they may be gram variable. With the Giemsa stain they take on a blue color. They may grow in a wide pH range, from 4.5 to 10. They grow as anaerobes under phototrophic conditions, as aerobic heterotrophs, or as microaerophilic, with a 10 percent carbon dioxide supplement. The growth is faster as microaerophilic with carbon dioxide, and the production of pigment is higher under microaerophilic phototrophic conditions.

The studies of the physiology and morphology of the *Leobacillus rubrus* showed that, phenotypically, it is similar to some species from the *Acetobacter* genus. They are gram negative–gram variable, grow singly, in pairs, or in filaments, and produce an antifungal. They grow at a wide pH, starting in the acid side, and belong to the alpha group of the purple nonsulfur bacteria. Recently they have been classified as belonging to the alpha-Proteobacteria.

The *Acetobacter* bacteria are important metabolically. They grow in, and they produce, vinegar (acetic acid). It is an interesting coincidence that Jesus of Nazareth was offered vinegar in a sponge before his death. Genotypically (16S rRNA), the *Leobacillus* is closest to the *Beijerinckia* genus. The Beijerinckia are heavy producers of plastic as cellular inclusions in the form of reserve polymers. They are nitrogen and ammonium fixers, and they produce acetic acid. The property of nitrogen fixation is important in the conservation of the Shroud of Turin. (Some people have wrongly advised conserving the Shroud in an oxygen-free environment replaced by nitrogen. If this is done, however, those bacteria which are nitrogen fixers will grow out of balance, a catastrophe for the Shroud.)

The taxonomy of these gram-negative bacteria was studied using the cell fatty acid composition and the nucleotide sequence of the 16S rRNA. A dendrogram was constructed. These gram-negative bacilli were found to have the oligonucleotide sequence AAAUUCG, which is diagnostic of the alpha group of the Proteobacteria, and can be placed between the *Beijerinckia* and the *Rhodopseudomonas* genera. The name *Leobacillus rubrus* was given to this new genus and new species. The GC content is 55.5 percent. If we use the old classification, the *Leobacillus rubrus* will be an anoxygenic phototrophic purple nonsulfur bacterium with a GC content of 55 percent. The cell fatty acid study indicates again a new taxa of the purple nonsulfur bacteria.

ACETIC ACID. Phenotypically, the *Leobacillus rubrus* resembles the acetobacter bacterium. Both were classified in the alpha group of the purple nonsulfur bacteria. Both are gram negative or gram variable, grow as single cells, in pairs, or in long filaments. Both grow at a wide pH range, starting in the acid side, and both may produce an antifungal substance.[10] The acetobacter bacteria were named for their growth and production of acetic acid (vinegar). There are four main species of acetobacter,[11] each with several strains, and each species has a different percentage of GC or guanine and cytosine in its nucleotides: *Acetobacter aceti* has a GC content of 55.9 to 59.5; *Acetobacter liquefaciens* has a GC content of 62.3 to 64.6;

Acetobacter pasteurianus has a GC content of 52.8 to 62.5; *Acetobacter hansenii* has a GC content of 58.1 to 62.6.

The GC content in the *Leobacillus rubrus,* as we have seen, is 55.5 percent, similar to the *Acetobacter pasteurianus.* A strain of *Acetobacter pasteurianus* known as *Acetobacter xylinum* is capable of producing cellulose.[12] This polymer is produced outside the cell membrane. The cellulose fibers initially form a pellicle[13,14] at the surface, which, after a few days, produces bacterial floculation.[15]

Without my realizing it, I have had more than fifty years of experience producing these acid bacteria. When I was a child, I used to brew a Mexican beverage in small jars. It was called *tepache* and contained pineapple peelings. The bacteria that grew on the surface of the liquid was known as *nata or madre* and produce acetic acid. If the Man on the Shroud is Jesus of Nazareth, I wonder whether there is a relation between the water and vinegar given to Jesus before his death and the presence on the Shroud of the *Leobacillus rubrus.*

ANTIFUNGAL. The *Leobacillus rubrus* was found to produce an antifungal substance that inhibits the growth of yeasts *(Candida albicans)* and molds *(Acremonium hyalinulum, Aspergillus fumigatus, Cladosporium spp.).* The antifungal substance causes changes in the conidiogenesis of *Aspergillus fumigatus,* giving rise to abnormal secondary and tertiary conidiophores and elongation of the fungal phialides. This phenomenon has been reported previously in the action of some antifungals on *Aspergillus fumigatus.*[16] The antifungal substance demonstrates once more the beautiful balance that the Shroud possesses to protect itself.

PINK PIGMENT. The pink color in the anoxygenic phototrophic purple nonsulfur bacteria is caused by bacteriochlorophyll-a, bacteriochlorophyll-b, and carotenoids. The carotenoids and the cytochrome-a in the bacterial cells have an absorption spectrum at the

Soret Band,[17,18] which was thought by some scientists to be unique to
hemoglobin.[19]

PLASTIC. After a segment of a Shroud thread was placed on
Sabouraud dextrose agar and left there for four months, the bacteria
on the surface of the thread fibers markedly increased the bioplastic
coating (PHA). The closest plastic to PHA is the manmade
Polypropylene (PP), which has a density of 0.905, differing from the
1.25 density of PHA.

Micrococcus luteus

The cells of the *Micrococcus luteus* are spherical, gram positive, and
grow as single cells, pairs, tetrads, or clusters. They do not grow in
filaments or chains. They are halotolerant (may grow in NaCl at a
concentration from 0 to 12 percent) and are usually present on human skin. Their presence on the Shroud of Turin is considered a
normal contaminant.

Extreme Haloalkaliphilic Bacteria

Bacteria that grow in environments with high sodium chloride concentrations and at a high pH were isolated from the Shroud. They
grow in cultures containing Natron (sodium carbonate). These bacteria were studied and classified by B. Tindall.[20, 21]

Fungi

I have so far isolated four different species of fungi belonging to three
different genera: (a) *acremonium,* (b) *aspergillus,* and (c) *cladosporium.* Eight small cleistothecia (fungi teleomorphs) were found on
the blood remnants from the Shroud's image of the occipital region.
One of these cleistothecia (woven like filaments) was stained using the
Wright's technique. It measures 0.23 mm in length and 0.16 mm in
width. The hyphae arrangement is similar to the teleomorph of Asper-

gillus, known as Eurotium. Other structures found inside the blood smears look like Acremonium microcolonies, others like Cladosporium with shield-shaped conidia at the attachment points and target-shaped conidia. A blood sample from the Shroud's image of the left hand has this type of conidia.

A NATURALLY PLASTICIZED TEXTILE

PART 2: A NATURALLY PLASTICIZED TEXTILE

ON MAY 18, 1993, I HAD THE OPPORTUNITY TO CUT A thread from one of the trimmings of the Shroud of Turin that had been removed on April 21, 1988, by G. Riggi. The feeling that I had was certainly different from how I feel when cutting an ordinary piece of linen. The sensation that I had, while using a pair of extremely fine scissors, was similar to that of cutting thin copper or plastic wire.

The Shroud's thread had a particular luster, which had previously been noted by Wilson: "The linen, although ivory-colored with age, was still surprisingly clean-looking even to the extent of a damask-like surface sheen."[1] When I studied the thread with the optical microscope, I noticed that the surface of the hand-spooned flax fibers was not uniform. There was a transparent coating on the surface that was irregular, with some areas thicker than others. It reminded me of the natural surface deposits I had studied on pre-Columbian artifacts, which I discussed at several meetings of the Society for American Archaeology.[2,3,4]

What is the transparent coating on ancient artifacts? Is it similar to the glossy deposits on ancient carved jades whose beautiful luster cannot be duplicated in modern times? It is a polyester produced by bacteria, as a reserve polymer, and deposited on the surface of ancient artifacts.

The Shroud of Turin is a naturally plasticized textile. The plastic (reserve polymer) deposited inside the bacteria has a well-known structure. It is a 3-hydroxyalkanoic acid, of which beta-hydroxybutyric is the most common. These lipoid materials are produced most profusely when the cells are subject to a nutrient deficiency. The beta-hydroxybutyrate and beta-hydroxyisovalerate as copolymers can be purchased, by industries, under the name Biopol.

The plastic produced by the *Leobacillus rubrus* is a chain of medium-length Polyhydroxyalkanoate (mcl-PHA). I have studied mcl-PHAs on such ancient artifacts as the clay bowls found at Apatzingan, in Michoacán, Mexico.

POLYMERS

The word *polymer,* meaning "of many parts," was coined by the Swedish chemist Berzelius in 1832, when knowledge of the chemical structure of molecules was still limited. There was much controversy about molecules, and many chemical reactions were used to determine their constituents and structure. On April 27, 1863, Pierre Eugène Berthelot described polymers at a meeting of the Chemical Society in Paris. It is considered the first scientific discussion on the subject.

In 1877, Alexander Butlerov, a Russian chemist, used the chemical compound Brome fluoride to polymerize olefins like propylene. Hermann Staudinger, who in 1953 won the Nobel Prize in chemistry,

used this research with halogen compounds as polymerization cata-
lysts and expanded on it. He reported:

> *There is a complete lack of systematic investigation of sub-*
> *stances producing the polymerization of unsaturated com-*
> *pounds and this is why we tested the most varied halogen*
> *derivatives, to see which induce the formation of high mo-*
> *lecular polymers.*

By 1950, Karl Ziegler had found that triethylaluminum, in the
presence of certain transition metal compounds, catalyzes the polymerization of ethylene to high polymers. In 1954, Giulio Natta used
the low-pressure polymerization technique for ethylene, discovered by
Ziegler, and was able to produce the polymerization of propylene. On
December 10, 1954, Natta submitted a paper to *The Journal of the
American Chemical Society* on his work in synthesizing linear crystalline polypropylene. The configuration of polypropylene is such that
all the asymmetric carbons have the same configuration, with a crystalline structure formed by the spiralization of the chain molecule.
Natta suggested the term *isotactic* for the regularity in the construc-
tion of the polymer.

I offer the above information about polymers produced in the
laboratory so that the reader will understand that the natural polymer, PHA, that protects the fibers of the Shroud of Turin has better
characteristics than the synthetic polymers.

PLASTICS

Plastics are substances that can be molded or shaped, by a particular
technique, and will retain the new form. The best definition of plastics
was given by Yarsley and Couzens in 1968: "A plastic is an organic
material which on application of adequate heat and pressure can be

caused to flow and take up a desired shape, which will be retained when the applied heat and pressure are withdrawn."[5]

The plastic materials used in industry during the last century were derived from natural substances. For example, in 1839, Charles Goodyear obtained rubber from a tree and fixed it by the process named vulcanization. Nitrocellulose was discovered by Friedrich Schonlein in 1846; celluloid (or Parkesine) was discovered by Alexander Parker in 1862; and the plastic casein was discovered by W. Kirsche in 1897. Not until this century was a wholly synthetic plastic discovered. In 1909, the Belgian chemist Leo Baekeland used a reaction between phenol and formaldehyde to produce a new compound, subsequently called Bakelite.

BIOPLASTIC COATING

My first finding, in my study of the surface deposits on the fibers of the Shroud, was that the coating was organic. This was proved by the first test, infrared spectroscopy (FT-IR).

As I said earlier, the reserve polymers that the *Leobacillus rubrus* accumulates are polyesters of the polyhydroxyalkanoate type (PHA). These alpha-proteobacteria produce the medium-length chain polymers (mcl-PHA). The simplest PHA molecule is the polyester of the beta-hydroxybutyric acid, which was first reported by M. Lemoigne in 1926 in *The Bulletin of the French Chemical Society*. The most important aspect of PHA is that it is biodegradable.

NATURALLY PLASTICIZED TEXTILES

Rosalie David, in her book *Mysteries of the Mummies,* describes the process of mummification:

The body was cleansed and rinsed through with palm wine and crushed incense: it was then filled with crushed myrrh, cassia, and other spices and sewn up again. It was then preserved by means of natron, although there is some controversy over the method actually employed. It was originally thought that the bodies were actually immersed and soaked in baths of natron, but it is also possible that dry natron was used.[6]

David goes on to describe natron:

Natron, the main chemical agent in mummification, is a salt mixture occurring in natural deposits. Samples from modern deposits show a large proportion of sodium carbonate and sodium bicarbonate, more commonly known as washing soda and baking soda respectively.[7]

STUDY OF THE COATING ON TWO EGYPTIAN MUMMIES

To understand the effect of the plastic coatings on the radiocarbon dating of ancient textiles, I studied the textile of two Egyptian mummies, one from the Manchester Museum, and the other an ibis bird in my private collection.

MANCHESTER MUMMY NUMBER 1770

The Manchester Mummy 1770 probably came from the excavations of Sir Flinders Petrie (1853–1942) and has been in the museum since the 1890s.[8] The mummy is that of a thirteen-year-old girl, unwrapped on June 10, 1975, by a team directed by Rosalie David.[9] The mummy bandages were badly preserved. The external bandages were in the form of strips and the inner ones in the form of fabric sheets made of flax *(Linum usitatissium)*. The diameter of the flax fibers was between

12 and 30 micrometers. In comparison with the modern linen fibers, the fibers from the mummy 1770 have a thickened wall and narrow central cavity.[10] Most of the textile was a double weave (double threads in both the warp and weft) and a small part of the textile in a plain weave.[11]

Several radiocarbon measurements were carried out by Dr. G.W.A. Newton, from the Chemistry Department of the University of Manchester. These measurements were done on the wrappings as well as bone from the mummy, and the radiocarbon results were different.[12] The radiocarbon age of the bones was 3161 B.P. (1510 B.C.), the radiocarbon age of the wrappings was 1758 years B.P. (A.D. 255), a difference of more than 1500 years.

In January 1996, Dr. David traveled to San Antonio, Texas, for the First International Symposium on Archaeomicrobiology. She brought me some samples of the mummy 1770 wrappings, which I studied with the optical microscope. I discovered that the flax fibers have a heavy coating of bioplastic, similar to coatings I have found on other ancient textiles, but this coating had a red tint, which needs further study.

Egyptian Ibis Mummy

The mummy of the ibis was also studied at the Symposium on Archaeomicrobiology, and the presence of a bioplastic coating on its flax fibers was established. A 6 Molar sodium hydroxide solution was used to dissolve the cellulose from the flax fibers, and the flax fibers were dissolved by the extreme alkaline solution. The bioplastic coating remains (was left as empty tubes) after the cellulose was destroyed.

The samples taken by Dr. Rosalie David for radiocarbon dating came from a bone and from a piece of dry muscle in the leg, as well as from wrappings. They were hand-carried by Dr. Douglas Donahue to the radiocarbon facility of the University of Arizona at Tucson, where four measurements were made:

1. Wrapping from the mummy cleaned with the acid-base-acid technique and washed with distilled water: 2255 +/– 75 years B.P.
2. Wrapping from the mummy cleaned with acetone, followed by the acid-base-acid technique: 2200 +/– 55 years B.P.
3. Collagen from the bone of the ibis: 2680 +/– 50 years B.P.
4. Collagen from tissue near the bone of the ibis: 2570 +/– 80 years B.P.

The results showed that the wrappings were 400 to 700 years younger than the ibis bone and tissue. Some scientists who work on radiocarbon dating have suggested that the discrepancy was due to the ibis's diet, based on fish from the bottom of the Mediterranean Sea.

The delta 13C for the collagen of the bone and tissue in the ibis mummy was of –21 per mil, and for the ibis wrappings was of –26.5 per mil. Both numbers are very different from marine samples that have a delta 13C value of zero. This proved that the ibis was not fed fish from the bottom of the Mediterranean Sea.[13]

Before the radiocarbon measurements were made, I told Dr. H. Gove that a difference of at least 500 years between the ibis collagen and the ibis linen wrappings would suggest that the bioplastic coating was an unsuspected contaminant. And, indeed, the results indicated that discrepancy. It was similar to the one in the Manchester Mummy 1770.

The bioplastic coating on the linen fibers of the Shroud of Turin is thicker than the bioplastic coating on the Manchester Mummy 1770 and the bioplastic coating on the ibis mummy. The difference between the collagen and the wrappings of the ibis mummy was 550 years.

THE OFFICIAL
SHROUD PHOTOGRAPHS

I N 1898, TWO CELEBRATIONS WERE PLANNED IN THE CITY of Turin, at the Italian Piedmont: the fiftieth anniversary of the Constitution, and the marriage of Prince Victor Emmanuel, the son of King Umberto I, of the House of Savoy, legal owners of the Shroud since 1453. The king gave permission for pictures to be taken of the Shroud during the display scheduled from May 25 until June 2. The Archbishop Agostino Richelmy of Turin approved the decision,[1] and permission was granted to Secondo Pia, an amateur photographer with more than twenty-five years of experience.

Secondo Pia, who was born in Asti in 1855, started experimenting with photography in the 1870s. He learned how to produce his own glass plates and in 1890 won the Grand Gold Medal for his excellent photographs.[2] The previous Shroud display had been in 1868, and the Shroud had been undisturbed in its silver casket for the next thirty years. Secondo Pia, who was thirteen years old during that show, did not see the Shroud. He tried to learn details from those who had attended the display, but their recollections were vague.

The first problem Pia confronted in taking the photographs was the lighting, which was poor inside the Cathedral of St. John the Baptist. I thought of that problem during my visits to the cathedral in April 1998 and May of 1993, and realized how bad the lighting must have been for Pia, at a time when electrical power was not as stable as it is now. In his time, only a few buildings had electricity. After experimenting for a few weeks with artificial lighting, Secondo Pia decided to use two lamps, one on each side of the scaffolding on which he mounted his camera. That had to be level with the Shroud, which was above the main altar in the cathedral. Pia relied on translucent glass filters in front of the lamps to diffuse the light.[3]

His first attempt was at noon on May 25, 1898, when he tried a fourteen-minute exposure. The photographic plates were Edward's 50-by-60 gelatin-brome orthocromatic plates; he used a yellow screen and a Voigtlander lens with a 7-mm aperture. During the middle of the exposure time, one of the light diffusers broke under the heat emitted by the reflectors, and Pia had to stop. On May 28, he tried again, this time at eleven at night. He had found that the Shroud was protected by a heavy frame, with glass, on order of Princess Clotilde.[4] He took two exposures, fourteen minutes for the first and twenty minutes for the second. The Shroud was again illuminated by two electric lamps at a distance of ten yards. Pia took the two exposed glass plates to his home, near the cathedral.

At home, around midnight, he took the first plate negative out of the developing solution (iron oxalate) and, in the darkroom, lighted only by a small red bulb, he saw before him an image of the Man on the Shroud. He later said: "Turning the plate on its side, I gazed at the face, and what I saw made my hands tremble. The wet plate slipped, almost dropping to the floor. The face, with eyes closed, had become startlingly real."[5] He stayed "shut up in my darkroom, where I experienced a very strong emotion when, during the development, I saw for the first time the Holy Face appearing on the plate with such clarity that I was dumbfounded. No human being could have painted this negative, which lies hidden in stains . . . If it was not painted, not made by human hands, then . . . I was looking at the Face of Jesus."[6]

One of the people who had helped Pia obtain the necessary permits was Baron Antonio Manno, president of the Exhibition of Sacral Art in Turin in 1898. Early in the morning on May 29, 1898, Pia sent him a short report on the success of his picture. The *Corriere Nazionale,* a Turin newspaper, reported on June 2, 1898, "The photograph is stupendously successful and has an exceptional importance for religion, history, and science. But of this we shall speak later."[7]

The news of the positive image seen on the orthocromatic glass negative plates spread rapidly, and many members of Italian high society, together with dignitaries from the church, visited Pia's house to see the photographs with their own eyes. The plates were exhibited in a darkened room, illuminated from behind. The figures were impressive. One of the visitors was Marquis Fillipo Crispoldi, who wrote a report in Genoa's newspaper *Il Cittadino,* on June 13, 1898: "The picture makes an indelible impression . . . the long and thin face of Our Lord, the tortured body and the long, thin hands are evident. They are revealed to us after centuries; nobody having seen Him since the Ascension into Heaven . . . I do not want to delay a minute in giving this news."[8]

Again, the *Corriere Nazionale* reported, on June 14, 1898:

Now that the indiscretion has been made, there is no further reason to keep secret the details of an event that will soon become of interest to all Christendom . . . The Redeemer, who miraculously left the imprint of His sufferings and the lines of His body on the funeral linen, reappeared on the glass miraculously outlined, with an amazing fineness of detail. There appeared the noble figure, anatomically elegant, perfect, divinely beautiful; the face still with an expression of ineffable pain and misery. And there appeared the details of the beard, of the hair, the profile, the scars, and the im-

*print of the rope with which the sacred body had been se-
cured to the column for flagellation. In short, after nineteen
hundred years, during which the world* CONTEMPLATED *the
figure of the Nazarene by the aid of tradition, the photograph of the Shroud has now given us a* PICTURE.[9]

The Vatican newspaper *Osservatore Romano* gave the news of
Pia's pictures on June 15, 1898, together with the official church
report on the Shroud findings.[10] The news was accepted, however,
with some skepticism, because this was a period during which many
unfounded reports about Christianity were being circulated.

After the publication of Secondo Pia's photographs, Ulysse Chevalier, a professor of ecclesiastical history at the Catholic Faculties of
Lyon, France, published his first article casting doubt on the Shroud.
"Le Saint Suaire de Turin est-il l'original ou une copie?"[11] was based
on a previous report, by Canon Charles Lalore, published on March 9
and March 16, 1877, in *Revue catholique du diocese de Troyes.*
Lalore, after examining all the documents from the fourteenth century regarding the Shroud, concluded that it was a fraud. He based
his judgment on a letter from Pierre d'Arcis to Pope Clement VII. This
letter was refuted in 1935 by Father Wuenschel in the *Ecclesiastical
Review*:

*Taken on its own merits, the memorial of Pierre d'Arcis is
untrustworthy because it was written in anger and betrays a
strong bias against Geoffrey de Charny and the Dean of
Lirey. Clement VII himself, in his reply to de Charny and in
his final decree, declared that Pierre d'Arcis was angry with
his opponents for obtaining a permit to exhibit the Shroud
without his permission.*

*He was even more angry when they ignored his com-
mand to withdraw the Shroud from worship by the public,
and he decried the king's intervention in preventing him*

from taking action against them. He was further hurt and humiliated when Clement VII upheld his opponents, and put him under silence, in the reply to de Charny, a layman, leaving the outraged bishop to learn of the censure from common report.

Pierre d'Arcis has become memorable for the violent outburst over his grievances and for the special pleading in his own defense. He is so intemperate in his language, so bitter in his statements against those whom he accuses of hindering him, and so reckless in imputing to them the basest motives that we cannot accept his unsupported statement that they were guilty of base fraud.[12]

PAUL VIGNON AND
HIS VAPOROGRAPHIC THEORY

The studies done at the beginning of the twentieth century by Paul J. Vignon on the physical description of the Shroud images were carried out during a period in the history of the Shroud, when disbelief in its authenticity was almost general, Canon Ulysse Chevalier, as we saw had reported on his research of documents from the Middle Ages, which led him to conclude that the Shroud of Turin was a fourteenth-century painting.

Between 1900 and 1902, Paul Joseph Vignon, a professor of biology at the Institut Catholique, in Paris, did his first scientific studies of the images on the Shroud. Dr. Vignon, born at Lyons in 1865, belonged to a wealthy family and, as a youth, had been more interested in sports than in science. His passion was mountain climbing.[13] During some of his ascents of the tallest mountains in France and Switzerland, Vignon was accompanied by a young priest named Achille Ratti, who later became Pope Pius XI.[14] Vignon was married in 1892 to an eighteen-year-old who did not share his passion for climbing. He had a nervous breakdown in 1895 and took up painting as part of his therapy.

In 1897, he was invited by Yves Delage, a professor at the Sorbonne and director of the Museum of Natural History, to work with him on *The Biological Year,* a magazine he had founded. It is not known when Paul Vignon first heard about the Shroud photographs taken in 1898, but we do know that in 1900 Yves Delage showed him copies of those pictures and asked him to do a scientific study of the matter. At the beginning of 1900, Vignon went to Turin and talked with Secondo Pia and with Baron Manno; Pia gave him copies of the glass negatives. Vignon learned that two other people had taken photographs; one was a Jesuit priest named Gianmaria Sanna Solaro, and the other a police lieutenant named Felice Fino, who had used a negative plate that was 21 cm by 27 cm.[15] In this picture, the Shroud is 13 cm. Both of these amateur photographers gave Vignon copies of their pictures.

Vignon first examined Pia's negatives under magnification and observed that none of the image areas looked as though paint had scaled off, despite the many instances of folding and unfolding and of rolling and unrolling the Shroud had undergone. Vignon used paint on linen, which he then rolled and unrolled, and in each case the paint scaled off and the pictures were destroyed. From these tests, Vignon concluded that the image on the Shroud was not a painting.

At the beginning of this century there were two popular hypotheses about the formation of the images. One group stated that they were formed by the blood left on the linen by the dead body of Jesus of Nazareth. The second group espoused a religious hypothesis, according to which the body of Jesus, at the moment of the Resurrection, released an electrical discharge from the suddenly recovered body. Vignon dismissed both hypotheses as unrealistic. He had stated from the beginning of his research that if the Shroud was authentic, the images on its surface had been formed by a natural process that could be explained by physical laws, and that, in time, the mechanics of formation would be understood.

With the help of two scientists from the Sorbonne, Vignon put on a false beard and smeared it and his face with pulverized red chalk.[16] A piece of linen was coated with albumen, and Vignon's colleagues covered him with the cloth and gently made certain that it touched all areas of the face. Where they checked the results with a camera, they found a grotesquely deformed face.

The images on the Shroud, like photograph negatives, have a reversal of tone. Vignon, an artist as well as a scientist, had difficulty believing that an artist of the fourteenth century could have painted a human figure *without seeing what he was doing.* The first hypothesis he tried was the *contact theory,* according to which the images on the Shroud could have been formed when there was direct contact between the linen and blood or other human fluids. In his first experiments, he found the images formed in this way were distorted and deformed. He also found that, though some of the Shroud images were faint, the proportion was accurate, with a harmony of the figures that could not be effected if an artist used pigments in any of the available techniques. For Vignon the figures on the Shroud were *impressions.* If the impressions on the Shroud could not be produced by painting or by contact, he concluded, "The impressions shown on the Holy Shroud have been spontaneously produced." He went on to say, "The impressions date historically from so far back that they can only have been the result of some spontaneous phenomenon. No one in the Middle Ages had the knowledge necessary for the production by handicraft."

IVES DELAGE'S PRESENTATION
TO THE FRENCH ACADEMY

Paul Vignon was so absorbed by his studies of the Shroud of Turin that he dedicated most of his life (from 1900 until his death, on October 17, 1943) to studying it. The first eighteen months were the most intense period. He worked at the laboratories at the Sorbonne in collaboration with E. Herouard and M. Robert of the faculty and with René Colson, a professor of physics at the École Polytechnique. Their findings were presented in a report by Professor Ives Delage to the French Academy of Sciences, at four o'clock in the afternoon of April 21, 1902. The title of the paper was "The Image of Christ Visible on the Holy Shroud of Turin."[17] Delage, a well-known professor of biology and zoology, was known to be an agnostic (a person who claims that man cannot know God). He did not believe in miracles or religious relics, but he did believe in the existence of rare natural phenomena. Vignon was present at the presentation during this informal weekly meeting of the academy, which published all the papers in the official report, *Comptes Rendus*.

Delage started his presentation by describing the observations made on the negatives taken by Secondo Pia in 1898. He mentioned the apparent reversal of tones in the negatives and showed the audience an enlargement of the picture of the face. He then explained why he and others at the Sorbonne decided to investigate the phenomenon, using the methods practiced in anatomy, chemistry, and physics. He discussed Vignon's research, concluding that the images on the Shroud could not be paintings, either done directly on the fabric or left by pigments that later reversed their colors. He also described the bloodstains, the wounds produced by the nails in the wrists, the surprising nudity of the figures, and the harmony of the entire body, whose face was realistic and perfect, without any weakness. He said:

For these and other reasons, our conviction is that the image of the Shroud is not a painting made by a human hand but has been created by a physical-chemical phenomenon. The scientific question that presents itself is how a corpse can make an image, on the Shroud that covers it, in such a way as to reproduce its shape with the details of the facial features.

He further described the experiments done by Vignon and Colson showing that the image was apparently an orthogonal projection of the body, with the intensity of the impression at each point inversely related to its distance from the corpse, finally disappearing when the distance was more than a few centimeters. Delage then said:

Must I mention the identification of the person whose image appears in the Shroud? . . . The truth could be reached by two separate lines of inquiry. On the one hand, there was the story of Christ's Passion, telling plainly of a man who had suffered those very punishments. Is it not reasonable to bring together these two series of events and tie them to the same object?

After a brief rest, Delage continued:

Let us add that, in order for the image to have formed itself without being ultimately destroyed, it was necessary that the corpse remain in the Shroud at least twenty-four hours. This is the length of time needed for the formation of the image— at most, several days—after which putrefaction sets in, destroying the image and finally the Shroud.

In the studies performed for this book, I found that the time required for the formation of an image of biological origin was hundreds of years. This finding was confirmed by the images formed by organic remnants in pre-Columbian artifacts.

Delage's presentation at the Academy of Sciences concluded with the following strong words: "Tradition—more or less apocryphal, I would say—tells us that this is precisely what happened to Christ; dead on Friday and disappeared on Sunday." And he solemnly added: "The man on the Shroud was Christ."

Delage's presentation lasted about thirty minutes and the reaction to his report was harsh. The permanent secretary of the Academy of Sciences, M. Berthelot, refused to publish Delage's paper in the Academy's bulletin.[18] The press also distorted the report in its articles. France, at the beginning of the century, proved a hostile environment for the Shroud. Even Catholic scholars gave more attention to Chevalier's historical findings than to the research by Vignon and his colleagues. The press accused Delage of having betrayed the spirit of Science. In reply Delage sent an open letter to Charles Richet, director of the *Revue Scientifique,* who published it, together with a summary of the paper, in his periodical.

THE 1931 SHROUD PHOTOGRAPHS

During the celebration of the wedding of Crown Prince Umberto of Italy and Princess Maria Jose of Belgium in 1931, there was a new Shroud exhibition. It opened on May 3, 1931, and lasted for twenty-four days. The Archbishop of Turin, Maurilio Cardinal Fossati, with the approval of King Victor Emmanuel, commissioned Giuseppe Enrie, a photographer and the editor of the journal *Vita Fotografica Italiana,*[19] to take new photographs of the Shroud. On the first day of the exhibition, May 3, 1931, at eleven P.M., in the presence of Secondo Pia (now seventy-five years old) and Paul Vignon (sixty-five years old), Giuseppe Enrie took a test exposure. He carried the plate to the sacristy, where he had improvised a darkroom, and Pia and Vignon were present through all the stages of Enrie's development of the test plate. When the face of the Man on the Shroud appeared, Pia once again felt the emotion that he had felt thirty-three years earlier in his own darkroom. Enrie took the plate to Cardinal Fossati. Later Enrie wrote: "I will remember as one of the most beautiful moments of my life, certainly the most moving of my career, the instant in which I submitted my perfect plate to the avid look of the Archbishop and that whole select group of people."[20] After the presentation to the Archbishop, Enrie returned to the Shroud and took six more plates, without using protective glass. It was twelve-thirty when he finished his last plate. On May 21, 1931, Enrie took three more plates; on May 22, he took three more. As in 1898, several private photographs were taken in 1931, but they were not recognized officially.

In all, Enrie took four photographs of the entire Shroud, three each from a third of the Shroud, one from the complete dorsal imprint, one of the face and bust, one of the face at two-thirds its natural size, one of the face at its natural size, and a direct sevenfold enlargement of the nail wound in the left wrist. This enlargement was described carefully in the following way:

> But it was in the sevenfold enlargement of the wrist area that the scholars found the most important unassailable new fact: THE INDIVIDUAL THREADS of the material could be seen clearly, as well as the depressions between them, and there was no trace of coloring matter. Pigmentation inevitably would have filled the depressions and resulted in massed patches, under which the threads would be united and hidden. Yet each thread remained separate and individual. The image was an ineffably delicate suffusion of discoloration in the threads.

THE 1933 SHROUD EXHIBITION

In 1933, at another exhibition of the Shroud of Turin, no official photographs were taken, but when the Shroud was exhibited outside the cathedral at the end of the exhibition, the Shroud was photographed in daylight by hundreds of people. These photographs were not official.

THE 1969 SHROUD PHOTOGRAPHS

On June 16 and 17, 1969, Michele Cardinal Pellegrino, Archbishop of Turin, formed a committee of experts to study the Shroud and obtain information on the best way to preserve it. The photographs were taken by Giovanni Battista Judica-Cordiglia, son of Professor Giovanni Judica-Cordiglia. He used both a 35-mm camera and a 125-mm camera, and took a total of thirty-nine photographs in color and in black and white. Judica-Cordiglia described the techniques that he used in the report of the Commisione de Esperti. The photographs were also studied, in October 1973, by Dr. Max Frei, Dr. Robert Spigo, and Professor Aurelio Ghio, whose report was of great importance. Many further studies of the Shroud were done on the basis of the photographs taken by Pia, Enrie, and Judica-Cordiglia. The studies all stated that the negatives showed no sign of alteration; and the studies themselves were carried out under completely scientific conditions.

The apparent reversal of image on the Shroud photographs might lead us to believe that the Shroud itself acts as a negative. This is not true, even though parts of the body that should be light in a black-and-white photograph are seen as white in the negative, and even though the blood is also clear, as it is supposed to be. As I explained before, the deposits by bacteria of iron and manganese oxide in the bioplastic coating on the Shroud contribute to this apparent contradiction.

The images on the Shroud, when examined closely, are not well defined. I had the opportunity to see the Shroud directly on April 18, 1998, when I studied it carefully for more than an hour. The image contours are diffuse, without any definite borders. This phenomenon is consistent with the biological origin of the image; many ancient artifacts on which the action of bacteria and fungi can be seen act in the same way. The reason the deposits are not better understood is that there has been no serious study of the natural deposits produced by biological activity.

The frontal and dorsal images on the Shroud are like mirror images: the right side of the body is seen on the left side of the Shroud, and the left side is seen on the right. In the negatives, however, this is reversed. When you see a picture of a negative of the Shroud, the left side of the body is on the left side of the negative, and the right side is on the right. For purposes of study, this visual normalization in the negatives helps in explaining the lesions represented on the Shroud.

A report given by Noemi Gabrielli, former director of the Medieval and Modern Art Galleries of Piedmont, stated that the figures on the Shroud were neither of a biological nature nor a painting. Her explanation was that the Shroud was a medieval painting produced by an unknown method. Gabrielli later stated that, since artists in the fourteenth century did not understand perspective and did not know the stamping techniques of the later Renaissance, the Shroud presently in Saint John's Cathedral is not the same one seen at Lirey in the fourteenth century; that is, the Shroud of Turin is a copy of the Shroud displayed in Lirey.

Gabrielli's hypothesis was directly opposed to the one put forth by Vittorio Viale at the First National Congress for the Study of the Shroud of Turin, held in Turin in 1939. Viale reported that since in the Shroud studies he was not able to catalogue the Shroud as being in any particular art style, he had to conclude that the Shroud was not the work of a human artist.

THE 1973 SHROUD EXHIBIT

On November 23, 1973, the Shroud was displayed on Television and could be seen all over Europe. On November 24, a committee of experts were able to study some threads that were removed from the Shroud for their work. Professor Mari and Professor Rizatti received some, as did Professor Filogamo and Professor Zina. Professor G. Raes received, in addition to two threads, two samples from the Shroud, one 40 mm by 13 mm, and one 40 mm by 10 mm.

AN ACCELERATOR-BASED
MASS SPECTROMETRY

BY HARRY E. GOVE

PREPARED BY H. E. GOVE, SEPTEMBER 6, 1997

NUCLEAR STRUCTURE RESEARCH LABORATORY
UNIVERSITY OF ROCHESTER, ROCHESTER, NEW YORK

AN IMPORTANT PRACTICAL USE HAS BEEN MADE OF AC-celerators that are normally employed for basic research on the properties of atomic nucleus. One such machine is the tandem electrostatic accelerator, which produces beams of energetic positive ions. These ions are used to penetrate the nucleus of atoms in a target, thereby inducing a variety of nuclear reactions whose detailed study elucidates the varied properties of the nucleus. A tandem accelerator begins by producing a negative ion (a neutral atom to which an extra electron has been attached). Most elements in the periodic table readily form stable negative ions. These ions are attracted to the positive terminal of the accelerator through an evacuated tube and arrive there with velocities that are 2 to 3 percent of the velocity of light (which travels at a velocity of 186,000 miles per second). Inside the positive terminal, the ions pass through a thin foil or a gas-filled canal, where they suffer collisions with the atoms of the foil or gas. In these collisions, they lose several electrons in addition to the extra one that made them negative; that is, they change from singly charged negative ions to multiply charged positive ions. They are then accelerated away from the terminal through the second half of the tandem and arrive back at ground potential traveling even faster (with velocities closer to 10 percent of the velocity of light). At this stage they are accurately energy-analyzed and directed toward the target by magnetic and electric-deflecting fields. The whole system acts like a very special mass spectrometer, although it is normally not used for measuring the masses of the ions it accelerates.

It can be so used, however, but the question is: Why would anyone want to? What are its advantages over conventional mass spectrometers? To answer this question, consider the field of radiocarbon dating. Stable carbon occurs with two masses, one (carbon-12) has 6 protons and 6 neutrons in its nucleus, and the other (carbon-13) has the same number of protons but has one more neutron. There are several unstable or radioactive forms of carbon, one of which is carbon-14. Its nucleus has 6 protons and 8 neutrons. It is often called radiocarbon, although all the unstable forms of carbon could also be called radiocarbon. Carbon-14 is particularly interesting because it lives a long time; it has a half life of 5730 years. That means that if one had a hundred atoms now, there would be only fifty 5730 years from now and only twenty-five in a further 5730 years, and so on. Carbon-14 is formed in the atmosphere by the interaction of cosmic ray neutrons with nitrogen-14 in the air. Like the two stable isotopes of carbon in the atmosphere, it quickly joins with oxygen to form carbon dioxide gas. The combination of its formation by cosmic rays and its death by radiocarbon decay causes an equilibrium to be established with the stable atoms of carbon. If one could examine a trillion carbon dioxide molecules from the atmosphere, most would be made from carbon-12, 10 billion (1 percent) would be made from carbon-13, and only *one* would be made from carbon-14. That is the equilibrium ratio mentioned above. Since all living things (plants and animals) ingest carbon dioxide, all living systems have this equilibrium ratio of unstable carbon-14 to the stable forms of carbon. When a living system dies, however, its intake of carbon dioxide ceases. The stable carbons stay unchanged, but carbon-14 continues to decay and is no longer replenished. A biological system that died 5730 years ago has only half as much carbon-14 (compared with its complement of stable carbon) as living systems have today.

Clearly, the length of time a biological system has been dead can be determined by measuring the ratio of carbon-14 to the stable carbon in the system. The straightforward way of doing this is to convert the carbon in the system to a gas—for example, carbon dioxide— place the gas in a counter that can detect the electrons that are emitted when the carbon-14 decays, and measure the counting rate. This counting rate is directly proportional to the number of carbon-14 atoms in the sample. A comparison with gas samples made with carbon of a known age—for example, contemporary carbon—can readily establish the age of the unknown sample. Willard Libby won the Nobel Prize for Chemistry in 1960 for recognizing this.

The disadvantage of radiocarbon-decay counting is related to the long half life of carbon-14. Very few of the carbon-14 atoms in a sample will decay in a finite counting period. For example, if one converts one gram of carbon from a contemporary biological sample to gas and then uses it to fill a counter, it would take a day to register the thousand counts (the number to get a dating accuracy of 1 percent or +/– 80 years). In this time only one ten-millionth of the carbon-14 in the sample would have been measured, and that is low efficiency. If one tried to use a smaller sample size—say, one hundred times smaller—it would take over two months of counting to produce a similarly accurate date.

It had long been hoped that a method could be found to detect carbon-14 directly by a technique that did not depend on its radioactive decay. Mass spectrometers seem the obvious answer. They are devices that generally start with positive ions, accelerate them to a modest velocity, and then, using a combination of magnetic and electric fields that bend the particles by an amount proportional to their mass, separate the ions of different masses from one another. The problem is that a variety of positive ions from a sample to be carbon-dated have masses close to that of carbon-14. These are nitrogen-14, whose mass is the same as carbon-14 to one part in a hundred thousand, and mass 14 molecules, hydrides of carbon-12 and carbon-13 whose masses differ from carbon-14 by one part in a thousand or so. For a mass spectrometer to separate minuscule amounts of carbon-14 from these other prodigiously abundant mass 14 ions would require a design that would have to be inherently inefficient. Major efforts to design such a device have been made but have failed.

The use of a tandem electrostatic accelerator at once solves both of the problems mentioned above. Nitrogen-14 is one of the few elements that does not form stable negative ions, while all types of carbon atoms do so readily. Hence, no nitrogen-14 ions are produced in the negative ion source, and the problem with the worst of the interfering ions is solved. The second problem, that of mass 14 molecules (e.g., 12CH2 and 13CH), is solved in the terminal of the accelerator during the process in which the ions are converted from negative to positive. It has been shown that if three or more electrons are removed from a neutral molecule like CH4, the carbon and hydrogen components of the molecule can no longer hang together. The resulting molecular fragments are readily distinguished from carbon-14 at the high-energy end of the system.

At the high-energy end of the accelerator, the multiply charged positive ions are passed through combinations of magnetic and electric fields. These serve to select ions of a specific ratio of mass to charge and of a unique velocity, and the particles then pass into a gas-filled counter. The counter is designed to measure the rate at which the particles lose energy as they collide with the gas atoms in the counter. This provides an additional piece of information about the particles, namely, their atomic number (the atomic number is the number of protons in the atomic nucleus or the number of electrons which circle the nucleus of the neutral atom). Although this information is redundant in the case of carbon-14 measurements—where it is not necessary to distinguish the atomic number of 6 for carbon-14 from that of 7 for nitrogen-14—there are situations involving other radioisotopes for which it is important.

In the early measurements made in May 1977 at the University of Rochester's Nuclear Structure Research Laboratory by a team of scientists from that laboratory, from the University of Toronto, and from the General Ionex Corporation, samples of very old carbon (petroleum-based graphite) and young carbon (hardwood barbecue charcoal) were measured. It was estimated that the overall efficiency of the system (fraction of carbon-14 in the sample actually counted at the high energy end) was 0.1 percent. This is ten thousand times more efficient than the radiocarbon decay–counting method. In these initial tests it was also shown that a small background of carbon-14 in the system caused the apparent age of the petroleum-based graphite to be 65,000 years (it is actually billions of years old). This is, however, somewhat better than can be done by radioactive decay counting, because of the background produced in the counters by cosmic rays.

It is the small sample size, however, that excites the practitioners and users of radiocarbon dating. Carbon sample sizes as small as a ten thousandth of a gram have been successfully measured at Rochester, and samples of a few thousandths of a gram are routine. This opens up a tremendous new field of dating possibilities in geology, archaeology, and anthropology, to name a few fields. In particular, it means that archaeological and anthropological artifacts can now be dated virtually without affecting the integrity of the artifact. A few examples may be of interest. A human skeleton—Del Mar Man—was uncovered near Del Mar, California. A type of dating method called amino-acid racemization suggested that the skeleton was 50,000 years old, which would be startling if true. This dating method is still somewhat controversial, and a radiocarbon date would be valuable. To be believable, however, the sample to be dated should be carbon from certain amino acids recovered from the bone, and only the new method could be used without destroying an appreciable portion of the skeleton. In another case, a possible—indeed, probable—Viking site was found at L'Anse aux Meadows on the northern tip of Newfoundland. A fire pit at the site had evidently been used for smelting iron, because iron slag was found in the pit. This already established that the site was used by Europeans, since the native population of North America were Stone Age people until fairly recently. Small carbon inclusions found in the slag undoubtedly came from the wood used in the fire. These samples are enough to date by the new accelerator technique, but not by radiocarbon counting. The site dated to about A.D. 1000. Finally, in 1977, a frozen woolly mammoth calf was unearthed from a peat bog in the Magadan region of Siberia. Soviet scientists provided a sample of muscle weighing 1.3 grams to a member of the anatomy department of Wayne State University. His studies showed, among other things, that whole red and white blood cells were contained in the sample. He provided the Rochester collaboration group with 70 milligrams (one four hundredth of an ounce) of muscle. A small amount of it was converted to about 18 milligrams of carbon and was measured in the University of Rochester's tandem electrostatic accelerator. Its age was found to be 28,000 years.

Since the first measurements were made at the University of Rochester's Nuclear Structure Research Laboratory in May 1977, some forty similar laboratories throughout the world have been working in this new applied physics field. Perhaps even more remarkable is the fact that there are many laboratories with small accelerators based on the Rochester system that was designed specifically for radiocarbon dating and similar measurements of other radioactive elements. The terminal voltage on large tandems can go as high as 14 million volts or so, but that is much higher than is needed for radiocarbon measurements. These dedicated systems have terminal voltages of only 2 to 3 million volts. Their cost is about three quarters of a million dollars each. They are able to deal with samples ten thousand times smaller than the conventional method requires; they will be able to do radiocarbon dating back to 65,000 years in time; and they will give radiocarbon dates that are accurate to plus or minus thirty years or less.

The cosmic ray flux of neutrons has not been constant through all time, so the production rate of carbon-14 has fluctuated. Some method of measuring the extent of this variation is needed. The Tree Ring Laboratory at the University of Arizona has been able, through the science of dendrochronology, to establish the true dates of individual rings of bristle cone pine back to 8000 years. There are living bristle cone pines that are 4000 years old and dead trees whose rings can be correlated with those in the living trees that go back a further 4000 years. By radiocarbon dating the wood of known age, one can obtain a calibration curve that will accurately correct radiocarbon ages. Measurements of carbon-14 have been carried out on bristle cone pine using wood samples containing ten tree rings and the conventional radiocarbon decay counting method, and they illustrate the importance of this calibration. For example, a true date of A.D. 1700 carbon dates as A.D. 1850, a true date of A.D. 0 carbon dates as A.D. 100, and a true date of 3640 B.C. carbon dates as 3000 B.C. Organic archaeological samples younger than 8000 years can now be accurately dated using sample sizes of a few milligrams, as required by the accelerator mass spectrometry technique, and by applying this accurately measured dendrochronological calibration curve.

THE CARBON
DATING OF
THE SHROUD OF TURIN

*It culminated in the only measurement that could provide
definite information on a fundamental property of the Turin Shroud, namely, the time when the flax used to make the
Shroud's linen was harvested.*

—H. E. GOVE 1996[1]

ON MAY 6, 1988, THE FIRST OFFICIAL SAMPLE OF THE
Shroud of Turin was radiocarbon dated at the University of
Arizona at Tucson. The results were not the expected ones. The sample showed that the Shroud of Turin was only 640 years old.[2] In his
book *Relic, Icon or Hoax?*, Harry E. Gove quotes D. Donahue as
saying that he did not care what results the other two laboratories
got; A.D. 1350 was the Shroud's age.[3] How the radiocarbon test on
the Shroud of Turin was done and how the age of the sample was
calculated with the data given by the accelerator mass spectrometry is
the clue to understanding the discrepancy in the age obtained from
the Shroud of Turin and the true age of the Shroud of Turin.

Many scientific reports have been given at meetings, and many papers published in journals, offering solutions for this discrepancy. The first point to keep in mind is that the radiocarbon people are honest scientists, and I am proud to be a friend of several of them. If there is an error in the age that is calculated by the interpretation of the data given by the AMS sample because of the presence of an unsuspected contaminant, it must be taken exactly as that. *An error caused by an unsuspected contaminant, and nothing else.* When you count the number of carbon-14 atoms present in a sample whose age you want to determine, you must compare it with the number of atoms of carbon-12 present in the same sample. The computer attached to the AMS has some tables that automatically give the probable age of the sample, using the relation between the two types of carbon. But if, after cleaning your sample, you leave an *unsuspected contaminant,* the result given by the computer is going to be wrong, and you will never notice this mistake. It does not matter how many statistical calculations you make or how many samples you use for your statistics: your result is going to be *unintentionally wrong.*

WHAT IS RADIOCARBON?

In the year 1960, Willard Libby received the Nobel Prize in Chemistry for his discovery of the applications of carbon-14 in the dating of ancient organic objects. Libby had been studying the quantity of the carbon isotope with the weight of 14 in organic products for over fifteen years. You may wonder exactly what the radiocarbon (carbon-14) is and what role it played in discrediting the Holy Shroud.

The matter that forms the universe, the inorganic elements as well as the organic, is composed of millions of particles called atoms. Atoms unite with other atoms, similar or different, to form the structure of the smallest quantities that make up a substance, that is, the smallest amount of matter. These small structures, the molecules, are the smallest units of matter that form the substances and compounds that constitute the universe. Now, atoms are also formed by different corpuscles of energy that are believed to comprise groups of vibrations. The three major corpuscles in an atom are: (a) the electrons, which are negatively charged, (b) the protons, which are positively charged, and (c) the neutrons, which, as the name suggests, are neutral and therefore have no charge. Electrons have such small weight that they are not taken into account, but neutrons and protons have similar weights, and these together are considered a unit.

There are ninety-two naturally occurring elements that form matter in the earth; there are also various elements that are not naturally occurring, which have been formed in the laboratory with an atomic number higher than 92 (uranium). To date there are twenty elements that have been made in the laboratory (atomic numbers 93 to 112). The elements 110, 111, and 112 (heaviest element at present) were produced at the Heavy-Ion Research Laboratory in Darmstadt, Germany. These elements were made for the first time in November 1994 (110), December 1994 (111), and February 1996 (112). Each element has its own atomic number, distinguishing it from the others. This number indicates how many protons (positive particles) exist in the nucleus (the central core of an atom). When the nucleus has one proton, we have the first element of the series, which is hydrogen, with an atomic number of one. This means that it has one proton in its nucleus, one electron (negative particle) rotating around the nucleus in an elliptical orbit called an energy shell, and no neutrons. Helium, which is an inert, or noble, gas, has an atomic number of two, indicating that it has two protons in its nucleus and two electrons rotating around the nucleus in opposing elliptical orbits. The series increases one by one, and each new element has its own name.

The atomic weight of the element indicates the sum of the protons and the neutrons in its nucleus. For example, carbon has an atomic number of six, but its weight can be twelve (carbon-12), thirteen (carbon-13), or fourteen (carbon-14), indicating that it can have six (C12), seven (C13), or eight (C14) neutrons in the nucleus besides the six protons. Remember that the number of protons cannot change in an element, because that would turn it into another element. For example, if we add one proton to the six protons in carbon, then it would be a new element, nitrogen, which has the atomic number seven.

Atoms with the same atomic number but different weight, like carbon-12, carbon-13, and carbon-14, are called *isotopes.* When an isotope is not stable—that is, if it becomes decomposed or self-destroyed over time—it is an *unstable isotope* or a *radioactive isotope.* This is true of carbon-14, which is unstable or radioactive.

The time it takes for the destruction of a radioactive isotope is different for each of the unstable or radioactive isotopes. The time needed to disintegrate half of the radioactive atoms in a sample has been used as a base for measuring the life of an unstable element; it is called the *half life.* In the case of carbon-14, 5730 years are needed for the disintegration of half the number of atoms, meaning, of course, that half of the original atoms survive. (Libby had initially calculated the half life of radiocarbon as 5568 years, which is 3 percent less than the correct half life.)

We saw that there are three carbon isotopes: carbon-12, carbon-13, and carbon-14. The last is the only one that is unstable (radioactive) and changes over time by itself. These three types of carbon exist in nature in different quantities. Carbon-12 comprises 98.9 percent of all carbon atoms, carbon-13 makes up 1.1 percent, and carbon-14 is only 0.000000000001.5 percent (1.5 part per billion atoms).

HOW RADIOCARBON IS FORMED

When cosmic rays, which have a negative value and almost no mass, similar to electrons, penetrate the atmosphere, they combine with nuclei of hydrogen (protons) and produce neutrons. The velocity of the neutrons slows and their temperature rises, and they are therefore called *thermic neutrons.* Since the neutrons themselves have no charge, they produce transmutations in the nuclei of the atoms with which they collide.

It has been calculated that cosmic rays produce about two **thermic neutrons** every second in each square centimeter of the earth's surface. When the thermic neutron crashes against the nitrogen nucleus, which has a weight of 14, it liberates a proton, and the nitrogen atom is transformed into a carbon atom with a weight of 14. When nitrogen, with an atomic number of 7 and a weight of 14, changes a proton for a neutron, the nucleus changes from nitrogen (7 protons) to carbon (6 protons), but since the neutron has the same weight as the proton, the new carbon atom has the same weight—14—that the nitrogen atom had before it changed. The two atoms of carbon-14 that are formed every second for every square centimeter of surface are mixed with the rest of the carbon in organic matter, in the carbonate deposits at the bottom of the ocean, and in the carbon dioxide of the atmosphere.

Carbon-14 is not stable. As we have seen, it disintegrates and has a half life of 5730 years. When carbon-14 is a component of the carbon dioxide also called carbonic anhydride and is similar chemically to the carbon-12/carbon dioxide, it is distributed in the atmosphere, where it is mixed with the carbon dioxide (carbon-12). This carbon dioxide is utilized by plants, through the process of photosynthesis, using chlorophyll, and by bacteria, through the Calvin cycle on autotrophic carbon dioxide fixation. It is also used in microaerophilic conditions in which are formed carbohydrates (sugars) and other organic matter necessary for the growth and energy of the plants and bacteria.

The newly formed organic matter incorporates itself into the biological chain that utilizes the carbohydrates formed during the photosynthesis in plants or autotrophic carbon dioxide fixation in bacteria

(Calvin cycle). These new organic systems incorporate in their metabolism the organic products that carry carbon-14.

While the organism is alive, it continues to accumulate radiocarbon at approximately the same velocity at which it destroys it; in other words, it is in equilibrium, conserving the same proportion of carbon-12 and of carbon-14 until the time it dies. Then, of course, the organism stops incorporating radiocarbon, so the proportion of carbon-12 to carbon-14 begins to change, as the latter is destroyed. This relation between the two carbons, when measured, is what indicates the time that has passed since the organism died.

From the practical point of view, we can imagine that the neutrons are formed by the union of a proton (+) and an electron (–), each of which neutralizes the other when they unite. At the same time, carbon-14, which is unstable and has 8 neutrons and 6 protons, is destroyed only with the production of a beta particle (an electron), which leaves the nucleus. When this happens, one of the neutrons of the carbon-14, having lost one of its negative particles (beta), is transformed again into a positive particle (proton). With this, the structure of the nucleus changes to 7 protons and 7 neutrons (the atom of carbon-14 has 6 protons and 8 neutrons), transforming itself again into nitrogen.

Of the total carbon, 93 percent is in the form of carbonates and is on the bottom of the ocean, 2.6 percent is in the form of humus on the terrestrial surface, 2 percent is in solution on the surface of the ocean, 1.6 percent is in the form of carbon dioxide in the atmosphere, and only 0.8 percent of the total terrestrial carbon is in the biosphere (carbon in living organisms). The concentration of carbon dioxide in unpolluted air at sea level is only 0.0345 percent.

TECHNIQUES FOR
RADIOCARBON ANALYSIS

There are at present two techniques for the quantitative analysis of carbon-14. One calls for the count of the beta particles (electrons) liberated at the disintegration of one of the unstable neutrons of carbon-14, with the consequent formation of nitrogen-14. Large quantities (grams) of the sample are needed for the study. The other method of quantitative analysis is mass spectrometry, which measures directly the number of atoms of carbon-12, carbon-13, and carbon-14. By this method, we can measure the relation between the number of carbon-12 atoms and the number of carbon-14 atoms. Much smaller quantities of the organic matter (milligrams) are needed for this technique, using two mass accelerators in tandem (TAMS). This was the method employed in the 1988 radiocarbon determination of the Shroud of Turin by the scientists in the Arizona, Oxford, and Zurich laboratories.

In mass spectrometry, the organic matter is burned and its carbon dioxide is collected and transformed, by a catalyzer, into a pellet of graphite. The pellet is placed in the accelerator and converted into gas, transforming the carbon atoms into ions, which accelerate at different velocities according to their weight. As a result, they deflect at different degrees in the mass accelerator and are counted in different places of the mass spectrometer.

I would like to emphasize again that the important factor in quantitative analysis through the mass accelerator is the relation between the number of atoms in carbon-12 and in carbon-14. If the sample contains several organic substances, the mass spectrometer will register the sum of all the atoms of carbon-12 and carbon-14 in each of them, without differentiating among them. The AMS will give the average of the carbon-14 in the mixture.

Counting the amount of the different types of carbon isotopes gives an average of the radiocarbon remaining in each component of the sample. This is why the age given by the radiocarbon tables of the sample from the Shroud of Turin is not the age of the cellulose of the linen; it is the average of the radiocarbon still present in the linen added to the radiocarbon of other substances on the Shroud (bacteria, fungi, and bioplastic). The accelerator mass spectrometer is unable to differentiate between the radiocarbon atoms (carbon-14) of each component.

RADIOCARBON MEASUREMENT OF
THE SHROUD SAMPLES

The radiocarbon measuring technique using accelerator mass spectrometry was developed in Rochester, New York, at the Nuclear Structure Research Laboratory. Harry E. Gove, Ted Litherland, and Ken Purser were the first to use the tandem AMS for counting carbon-12 and carbon-14. The earliest determinations were carried out on May 18, 1977, on two samples: a piece of modern charcoal and a piece of graphite.[4]

Time magazine, in its June 27, 1977, issue described the new technique for measuring radiocarbon to calculate the age of an organic artifact. In his book *Relic, Icon or Hoax?*, Gove mentioned that the first he learned of the Shroud of Turin was in a letter he received from David Sox in England, dated June 24, 1977, asking whether the new radiocarbon-dating procedure could be used to date the radiocarbon in the ancient cloth known as the Shroud of Turin.[5] The letter from Sox began Gove's enthusiastic interest in the AMS dating of the Shroud, an interest that became an obsession.

The Second International Symposium on the Studies of the Shroud of Turin was held in Turin in October 1978. The Shroud was displayed from August 27 until October 7, and Gove had a firsthand opportunity to see the Shroud and then participate in the symposium. In the July 21, 1978, issue of *Science Journal*, B. J. Culliton published

"The Mystery of the Shroud of Turin Challenges 20th Century Science."[6] Culliton's description of the cloth and its images are excellent. She mentioned possible scientific studies to be done after the October exhibit and concludes, "No final judgment will be possible until the cloth is accurately dated, and carbon-14 dating is at least a couple of years away."[7]

THE TURIN WORKSHOP OF 1986

The workshop held in Turin on September 29 to October 1, 1986 in preparation for the Shroud radiocarbon was conducted at the Seminario Metropolitano. It was organized by Cardinal Anastasio Ballestrero and chaired by Carlos Chagas, president of the Pontifical Academy of Sciences. The participants were: Alan Adler, Shirley Brignall, Vittorio Canuto, Paul Damon, Robert Dinegar, Douglas Donahue, Jean-Claude Duplessy, Jacques Evin, Mechthild Flury-Lemberg, Luigi Gonella, Harry Gove, Teddy Hall, Garman Harbottle, Robert Hedges, Stephen J. Lukasik, William Meacham, Robert Otlet, Giovanni Riggi di Numana, Enrico di Rovasenda, Michael Tite, and Willy Woelfli.[8]

The number of threads in each square centimeter of textile are twenty-six in the weft and thirty-eight in the warp. The area density is, on average, 23 mg/cm square. Keeping in mind that the cellulose is a collection of molecules of glucose, each of which has a molecular weight of 180, with 6 carbons having a weight of 72, we can see that the ratio of carbon is 72/180 less the weight of the water molecule (18) removed in each glycosidic union. The workshop concluded that each square centimeter of the Shroud would produce around 5 mg of carbon. Of the seven radiocarbon laboratories to be used, the five ASM laboratories would need 25 mg of carbon, and the two small-counter laboratories would need another 25 mg of carbon. Those 50 mg of carbon were to be obtained from 10 cm of the Shroud's cloth.

At the end of the workshop, Carlos Chagas gave the following summary:[9]

1. This was the moment for carbon dating.
2. We would take the minimum amount of cloth needed to ensure rigorous scientific results and to ensure public credibility. This would not include charred material.
3. For statistical purposes it was decided that all seven laboratories were to be involved: the five accelerator laboratories and the two small-counter labs.
4. For logistical reasons, the samples would be removed immediately before the use of the Shroud by other groups for other experiments.
5. Samples would be taken, by Madam Flury-Lemburg, from areas devoid of other possible information content and outside the image.
6. Seven samples of the Shroud would be taken, and six Shroud plus one dummy sample would go to the seven labs.
7. The removal of the samples would be witnessed on closed circuit TV by representatives of the labs.
8. After the measurements were made, the results would be analyzed by the British Museum, the Turin Institute of Metrology, and by a third person or institution to be selected by the Pontifical Academy. The final analysis to be performed would have the participation of all the laboratories.
9. The radiocarbon groups would devise one method for reporting the data.
10. The threads of the samples would not be too short; each lab would employ its own method of cleaning.
11. Two control samples were to be supplied by the British Museum.

12. A press release, to be issued on Friday, would state that the samples were to be taken around May 10, 1987, and that the results would probably be made known to the public by April 1988.
13. Final results would be published as a collaborative enterprise.
14. No laboratory would charge for the time spent in conducting the measurement.
15. The certifying institutions (distributors) would be the British Museum (Tite), the Pontifical Academy (Chagas), and the Archbishopric (Gonella).
16. The analyzing institutions would be the Pontifical Academy, the Turin Institute of Metrology, and the British Museum.

On October 10, 1987, Cardinal Ballestrero sent a letter to each of the participants in the Turin workshop, notifying them that three laboratories had been selected for the radiocarbon test: (1) the University of Arizona at Tucson, (2) Oxford University, and (3) ETH, Zurich. Ballestrero mentioned in the letter some differences of opinion, and he concluded with a beautiful paragraph:[10]

> As we move on the executive phase of the project of radiocarbon dating the Shroud of Turin, I would like to thank again all those who brought positive contributions to it, and to offer my heartfelt good wishes to those who will undertake it, trusting that they will carry it out with utmost scientific rigor in order to add this important objective datum to the scientific quest that has long been growing on the illustrious image entrusted to my stewardship.
>
> —ANASTASIO CARDINAL BALLESTRERO,
> ARCHBISHOP OF TURIN,
> PONTIFICAL CUSTODIAN OF THE SHROUD OF TURIN.

In his book *Relic, Icon or Hoax?*, Gove published a letter from the three selected radiocarbon laboratories to Cardinal Ballestrero, an important document:[11]

> *Your eminence: We have received your letter of 10 October 1987, and we are honored to have been selected to participate in the age determination of the cloth of the Shroud of Turin. However, we are concerned to learn that a decision has been made to limit the number of participating laboratories to three. We are in agreement with the conclusions reached at the workshop held in Turin in September–October 1986 that: "a minimum amount of cloth will be removed which is sufficient to (a) insure a result that is scientifically rigorous and (b) to maximize the credibility of the enterprise to the public. For these reasons, a decision was made that seven laboratories will carry out the experiment . . ."*
>
> *We believe that reducing the number of laboratories to three will seriously reduce the credibility of the enterprise which we are also anxious to achieve. As you are aware, there are many critics in the world who will scrutinize these measurements in great detail. The abandonment of the original protocol and the decision to proceed with only three laboratories will certainly enhance the skepticism of these critics.*
>
> *While we understand your desire to use a minimum amount of material from the Shroud, we believe that the increased confidence which would result in the inclusion of more than three laboratories in the program would justify the additional expenditure of material. Although improvements in statistical errors resulting from including more measurements might not be great, the possibility of the occurrence of unrecognized nonstatistical errors would be substantially reduced.*

For example, if only three laboratories participate, and one of them obtains a divergent non-understandable result, the entire project could be jeopardized, but if results from a larger number of laboratories are available, a divergent result would be more easily recognized as such and be treated appropriately in a statistically accepted manner. Clearly it is the reduction of unrecognized nonstatistical errors in measurements that leads to increased confidence in the final result.

We would very much like to take part in the program to determine the age of the cloth of the Shroud, but we are hesitant to proceed under the arrangement in which only three laboratories would participate in the measurements. We urge that the decision to change the protocol of the Turin workshop and to limit participation to only three laboratories be given further consideration.

Respectfully

This excellent letter showed that the three selected radiocarbon laboratories shared a concern that there be a true, honest, and reliable test. But all these factors depended on the purity of the sample to be measured. If there was an unsuspected contaminant in the sample, as in the instance of the PHA polymer added to the Shroud of Turin (in the form of *naturally plasticized textile),* the result would be distorted. And those abnormal results would obtain if three or seven laboratories were involved.

After Cardinal Ballestrero's letter was received by the seven laboratories, Gove and Harbottle organized a press conference at Columbia University in New York on January 15, 1988.

The Turin newspaper *La Stampa* published an article on January 13, 1988, two days before the press conference, and Gove received an Italian to English translation of the *Stampa* article by Father Rinaldi.[12]

Two of the most prestigious American laboratories, Brookhaven's and Rochester's, do not accept their exclusion from the research program that aims to date the Turin Shroud. The archbishop and his research coordinator assert that "no official decisions have as yet been made" . . . With an "open letter" to the Pope, they will protest the recent decision of the Holy See and the Archbishop of Turin, Cardinal Ballestrero, to exclude them from the research.

The statement of the scientists of the two American laboratories will be made known at Columbia University on Friday, 15 January. Their open letter to the Pope, owner of the Shroud, will make the point that he is being "poorly advised" and that he is making a mistake if he approves a limited or reduced version of the research, whose outcome will be, to say the least, questionable. They ask the Pope to reconsider his decision and permit them to analyze fragments of the Shroud by the carbon-14 test . . .

How did the Turin archdiocese curia react to the protest of the American scientists? Said Cardinal Ballestrero, "It seems to me the U.S. scientists are acting as if the final decision has already been made. We are still discussing the situation and will in due time communicate the results." Rather cautious, too, is the reaction of Professor Luigi Gonella of the Turin Polytechnic Institute and supervisor of the Turin Shroud Research Project, Inc., a group of international experts who have been conducting research on the Turin Shroud for the last ten years. Says Gonella, "The Brookhaven and Rochester scientists have no reason to protest. There was no firm agreement with them. If anything, it was just a proposal. But aside from this, using a press conference to broadcast their protest is certainly not a laudable procedure. We hope that the serious business of research on

*the Turin Shroud will not end by becoming a race of who
can get there first."*

On January 22, 1988, members of the three selected radiocarbon
laboratories met in London. They were to organize the final preparation for the removal of the sample from the Shroud. After the meeting
a statement was released to the *Daily Telegraph*.[13]

*Representatives of the three radiocarbon-dating laborato-
ries, Arizona, Oxford, and Zurich, accepted by the Vatican
to undertake the radiocarbon dating of the Shroud met on
22 January at the British Museum, together with Professor
Luigi Gonella, the scientific advisor to the Cardinal of Turin, and Dr. Michael Tite of the British Museum, who had
been invited to help in the certification of the operation.
After discussion, they accepted the decision of the Vatican to
use no more than three samples, in the interest of conservation of the Shroud. Procedures for taking the samples from
the Shroud and for the treatment of the results were discussed, and proposals on this will be submitted to the Archbishop of Turin for his agreement. It is proposed that, as far
as possible, the spirit of the original protocol of the 1986
meeting be retained. Each laboratory will be provided with
control samples of known age. The samples will be taken
from the main body of the Shroud, away from patches or
charred areas, under the supervision of a qualified expert.
Certification of the samples will be undertaken by the Archbishop of Turin, Anastasio Cardinal Ballestrero, Pontifical
Custodian of the Shroud of Turin, and by Michael Tite of
the British Museum. Representatives of the three laboratories will be present in Turin to receive the samples. The overall procedures will be fully recorded by video film and photography. The laboratories will submit their results for*

statistical analysis to the British Museum and to the G. Colonnetti Institute for Metrology. The timetable for the operation has not been established, but it is hoped that the radiocarbon dates on the Shroud of Turin will be released by the end of 1988. If these proposals are approved by the cardinal, then a letter will be submitted to Nature, *giving further details of the procedure. The participants of this meeting wish to take this opportunity to record their appreciation to Professor Carlos Chagas, President of the Pontifical Academy of Sciences, who chaired the original meeting in Turin in October 1986, as well as the other participants who played a crucial role in moving the project forward.*

This is another excellent document on the plans for the dating of the Shroud. The statistical analysis was well planned, but, again, if an *unsuspected contaminant* was present, the result would be wrong no matter how many institutions were involved and how many statistical analyses were done.

The scientists who were not selected to participate in the research were sorely frustrated. In his book, Gove reported some of their thoughts: "A scientific investigation that could have been exciting and challenging and, above all, a great deal of fun, has turned sour."[14]

SAMPLES TAKEN FROM THE SHROUD

The samples were taken on April 21, 1988 at the Cathedral of Saint John the Baptist. Those present were Cardinal Anastasio Ballestrero, Luigi Gonella, Giovanni Riggi di Numana, Michael Tite, Damon, Donahue, Hall, Hedges, Woelfli, the two textile experts F. Testore and G. Vial, as well as the priests Monsignor Caramello, Monsignor Cavaglia, Monsignor Baldi, and Monsignor Luciano.

The first thing I noted about the sample-taking is that the Turin workshop of October 1986 appointed Madam Mechthild Flury-Lemberg, from the Abbeg-Stiftung Institute in Switzerland, to cut the sample. On April 21, 1988, however, that action was performed by Giovanni Riggi di Numana, who, together with Dr. Franco A. Testore, selected the area to be cut. The textile has a weight of 0.023 grams per square centimeter with thirty-eight threads in the warp and twenty-six threads in the weft in each square centimeter. The sample obtained from the Shroud was initially trimmed at the upper and lateral external borders, and the trimmings were set aside by Riggi and placed in a container sealed and stamped in wax by Gonella and Riggi.

According to Testore, the size of the sample after the initial trimming of the external borders was 81 by 16 mm, with a weight of 300 mg. This gives an areal density of 23.1 mg/cm square. Eighteen months after the sample was taken (on October 26, 1989), Testore mentioned that it was divided, following the trimming into two pieces, which were weighed on an electron scale from the Materials Department from the Polytechnic University in Turin; the scale was a Mettler model AE 166. When I visited Riggi in Turin on May 18, 1993, he told me that the first thing that he did to the sample was to trim the outside borders, which were heavily contaminated.

The large piece of cloth that remained after the trimming, was divided in two parts. Section A, with a weight of 154.9 mg, was retained by the Cardinal. Section B, with a weight of 144.8 mg, was divided into three segments of 52.0 mg, 52.8 mg, and 39.6 mg. These were the samples to be used by the radiocarbon labs. Unfortunately, because the samples assigned to the Arizona laboratory weighed under 50 mg (the one of 39.6 mg), a small segment (14.1 mg) was removed from the Cardinal's sample to complement the small piece. Arizona therefore received two pieces, one of 39.6 mg and one of 14.1 mg, for a total of 53.7 mg. The Cardinal's portion, Section A, was thereby reduced to 140.8 mg.

THE FIRST SHROUD SAMPLE DATED

The first sample was officially dated in Tucson, Arizona, on the morning of May 6, 1988. H. Gove was present. He wrote: "Based on these 10 one-minute runs, with the calibration correction applied, the year the flax had been harvested that formed the linen threads was A.D. 1350—the Shroud was only 640 years old!"[15]

I must correct this statement. Because the cleaning methods used in the laboratory did not remove the bioplastic coating, the sample was actually a mixture of organic materials with an average age of 640 years. But that was not the age of the flax, as Gove thought. I have explained this several times to Dr. Gove. Sorry, Harry!

Bill McClellan, a son-in-law of Donahue, wrote an article for the *St. Louis Post Dispatch* on May 15, 1988, entitled, "Secrets of the Shroud":

> *Donahue was the first person to read the results. The second was Harry Gove, who had been invited to Tucson by Damon and Donahue to observe the test.*
>
> *The evening of the day the Shroud of Turin was dated, Gove visited Donahue's home. The two men sat outside on the porch, enjoying the cool spring night. They talked about physics and mutual friends and the desert. Everything but the results of the testing of the Shroud of Turin.*
>
> *In the coming days the Tucson lab will be testing the other three pieces of its original sample of the Shroud. The results will then be sent to the British Museum, which is coordinating the tests. The other two labs will do the same.[16]*

REPORTS OF A FOURTEENTH-CENTURY FORGERY

Several newspapers published reports of rumors indicating that the Shroud was a medieval forgery. One, by Kenneth Rose in the London *Sunday Telegraph,* mentioned a medieval date.[17] The *Evening Standard* of August 26, 1988 carried a report by Dr. Richard Luckett, who said that the fourteen-foot piece of linen with what appears to be the imprint of Jesus has a date of 1350.[18] In the *Oxford Mail,* Hall contradicted Luckett's statement as "mere guesswork." He wrote, "The person who has been doing the dating told me that Dr. Luckett got the date completely wrong."[19] When Gove read Hall's response, he got the chills, he wrote: "The *Oxford Mail*'s report of Hall's response (that Dr. Luckett 'got the date completely wrong') to the 1350 date seemed to indicate that Oxford might have come up with a number quite different from Arizona."[20]

David Sox's book *The Shroud Unmasked* reports the medieval age of the Shroud. But according to Petrosillo and Marinelli, the book was printed in September 1988, before the official date was released by Cardinal Ballestrero.[21]

In the newspaper *Il Giorno,* on September 6, 1988, Gonella was quoted as saying: "If any researcher has spoken, it means that he took the trouble to verify which of the three samples delivered to each of the three laboratories came from the Shroud. We had trusted them; now we are disillusioned."[22]

CARDINAL BALLESTRERO ANNOUNCES THE RESULTS

The official radiocarbon date obtained by the three laboratories was released to the press by Cardinal Ballestrero on October 13, 1988.

Looking at ease in the hall of the Salesians at Valdocco, Turin, the Cardinal declared to the journalists:

With a dispatch delivered to the Pontifical Custodian of the Holy Shroud on September 28, 1988, through Dr. Tite of the British Museum, the coordinator of the project, the laboratories of the University of Arizona, Oxford University, and Zurich Polytechnic, which carried out the radiocarbon measurements of the fabric of the Holy Shroud, have finally communicated the results of their operations.

This document specifies that the interval of calibrated dates assigned to the fabric of the Shroud, with a degree of certainty of 95 percent, lies between A.D. 1260 and 1390. More precise and detailed information will be published by the laboratories and Dr. Tite in a scientific journal with a text that is being prepared.

For his part, Prof. Bray of the G. Colonnetti Metrology Institute of Turin, who was entrusted with the revision of the résumé presented by Dr. Tite, has confirmed the compatibility of the result of the three laboratories, whose certainty falls within the limits of the method employed.

After having informed the Holy See, the proprietor of the Holy Shroud, I am announcing what has been communicated to me.

While submitting to science the evaluation of these results, the Church confirms its respect and veneration for this venerable icon of Christ, which remains a cult object for the faithful in accordance with the attitude that has always been demonstrated towards the Holy Shroud, in which the value of the image is pre-eminent with respect to its possible value as a historical object, an attitude that refutes the gratuitous inferences of a theological character that were put forward within the sphere of an inquiry that had been presented as solely and rigorously scientific.

At the same time, the problems of the origin of the image and of its conservation still remain mostly unsolved and will demand further research and further study, towards which the Church will manifest the same openness, inspired by its love for truth, which it has shown in permitting the radiocarbon test, as soon as a reasonable working program is submitted.

The unpleasant fact that many news items relative to the scientific investigation have been anticipated in the press, especially in the English language, is a cause of personal regret to me, because it has favored the insinuation, certainly not an unbiased one, that the Church was afraid of science and concealed the results, an accusation that is the flagrant contradiction of the attitude that the Church, in this case, has firmly maintained.[23]

The *Osservatore Romano* published the statement of Cardinal Anastasio Ballestrero on October 14, 1988.

THE BRITISH MUSEUM PRESS RELEASE

The same day as Cardinal Ballestrero's press conference in Turin, the British Museum held a meeting for the press with Tite, Hall, and Hedges. On a blackboard behind the three speakers, who were sitting at a table, was written, in large numbers, the date "1260–1390!"

The spectacle reminded me of pre-Columbian times, when Maya warriors used to display, on the belts of their costumes, as if they were trophies, the heads of the enemies they had killed in battle.

The coincidence of the date given for the Shroud by the three radiocarbon laboratories and the first historical display of the Shroud in Lirey, France, was remarkable. At that moment no intelligent person would contest the date. Even if the date that the radiocarbon laboratories gave for the Shroud of Turin was not correct (because of the bioplastic coating that is an *unsuspected contaminant)* and some of the radiocarbon people acted like peacocks, I believe that they were honest in their mistake.

E. T. Hall published, in the February 1989 issue of *Archaeometry* (31:92–95), a paper entitled "The Turin Shroud: An Editorial Postscript." In it, he mentioned a few details that had been questioned:

(a) The test of the Shroud and two other (dummy) pieces of cloth was not a blind test. When opening the first of the three steel cylinders, it was obvious that it was indeed the Shroud sample on account of the distinctive weave which we had seen in Turin; no truly blind test could be attempted. However, after cleaning and burning the sample to carbon dioxide, the phials were relabelled with new numbers, the coding of which was not known to Dr. Robert Hedges whilst he was actually undertaking the measurements.

(b) It has been suggested that the fire of 1532 damaged the Shroud and that the carbon-14 content was altered by impregnation of modern carbon from burnt impurities; alternatively, that the cleaning procedures were inadequate and modern contamination altered the apparent date. Such suggestions are very wide of probability. (i) Tests on other pieces of burnt fabric showed no change of date even when scorching was severe. (ii) The amount of cleaning given to the Shroud was varied. There was no difference in the age obtained whether the portions were simply washed for the removal of gross contamination or strongly etched in acid and alkali. (iii) Assuming the Shroud sample was 2000 years

*old, the linen would have had to be contaminated with 40%
of modern carbon in order to give it a medieval date.*

*(c) Lastly, it has been suggested (somewhat in despera-
tion) that at the Resurrection, a high flux of neutrons was
produced which formed carbon-14 from local nitrogen. It is
somewhat surprising that the correct alternative date given
by the flux of neutrons was the fourteenth century—around
the time of the first reported exhibits of the Shroud.*

FIRST REACTIONS TO THE MEDIEVAL DATE OF THE SHROUD

The first reactions to the announcement of the medieval date of the
Shroud were as expected. Many people did not approve of the way
the news was given by Cardinal Ballestrero. In an interview with the
newspaper *La Voce del Popolo*, on November 6, 1988, the Cardinal
was questioned about his confidence in science.

*Because science asked us to trust it. And it is easy to realize
that science's accusation against the Church is always that
the Church is afraid of science, because the truth of science
is superior to the truth of the Church. Therefore, granting
an audience to science is, I think, a gesture of Christian
coherence. Living by the principle that "not trusting is better" is not Christian. I would like, however, to stress that
the Church has not accepted the results with its eyes closed.
The Church believed, even to liberate itself from an accusation of fear and disloyalty, that it should grant science a
hearing. Science has spoken; now science will pass judgment
on the results. Nobody has made me say that I accept these
results. I did not say it, and I am not saying it, because this
does not concern me. I am not a judge of science. That*

granting a hearing has not cost the Church anything is not true; but the Church is serene. It has affirmed and will continue to affirm that the cult of the Holy Shroud will continue and that the veneration of this Sacred Linen remains one of the treasures of the Church. And I must stress what I have already said many times: if the Shroud has entered the liturgy of a church, this is significant of its importance and its validity. The argument of science follows its own path. And it is most obvious that it is anything but exhaustive, with respect to the discernment on the Shroud of the image that evokes the face of Christ, and not just the face, and that recalls the mystery of the passion and death of Our Lord and perhaps also His Resurrection. And this is the reason for my serenity, even if, evidently, the interpretations given to the publication of the results have been seen sometimes as a "consensus" on the part of the Church. The Church never gave that, since it cannot give it nor should it give it. On this subject, I must also say that the news items recently broadcast about further investigations are not my concern. The present problem is to provide an adequate method for the conservation of the Shroud, a method that will guarantee the cloth the greatest possible security.[24]

William Meacham, one of the participants at the Turin Workshop on September 29—October 1, 1986, issued a press release in Hong Kong on October 14, 1988. It was published as follows:

TURIN SHROUD DATED TO A.D. 200–1000
IN SECRET TESTING:
Results Inconsistent with Recent Dates

A closely guarded secret testing of the Shroud of Turin in 1982 by an American carbon-14 laboratory yielded conflict-

ing dates of A.D. *200 and* A.D. *1000, an American archaeologist involved in Shroud research claimed today.*

Mr. William Meacham *of the University of Hong Kong said that members of the U.S. scientific team which examined the Shroud in 1978 informed him that a single thread was later tested at the University of California nuclear accelerator facility. He said separate ends of the thread gave quite different results, and the presence of starch was also detected during pretreatment. These findings were never published because carbon-14 testing did not have the approval of the Turin authorities at that time.*

He said Prof. L. Gonella, scientific adviser to the Archbishop of Turin, was only informed of the results in 1986, at a meeting which Meacham had attended.

Recently completed C-14 tests are reported to indicate a date of A.D. *1000–1500 for the relic, which bears the image of a male corpse with wounds of crucifixion. Extensive testing in 1973 and 1978 indicated that the image was a genuine body imprint with stains of human blood.*

Meacham said the recent C-14 tests proved nothing at all about the Shroud as a whole, since all three samples dated by Arizona, Oxford, and Zurich had been taken from the same spot on the cloth—a corner which had been scorched in the church fire of 1532.

"It is also possible that this area was re-woven by a medieval restorer, since it is just next to a selvage edge and side panel that were added to the Shroud some time after its original manufacture," he said.

The Shroud may not be one homogeneous cloth as far as its chemistry is concerned. We already know of significant variations from one point to another, and the radiocarbon content likewise may vary significantly.

The recent testing was very poorly planned. It is aston-

ishing that samples from at least two or three different points on the cloth were not taken for dating. Archaeologists who make frequent use of C-14 results are accustomed to samples occasionally giving aberrant results, and would normally not attach much importance to a single date, or, in this case, three dates on a single spot.

Meacham said he had repeatedly urged Gonella not to rely on one single site for dating the Shroud, especially in view of the previous test results from the California lab.

Criticism of Gonella surfaced earlier this year when four of seven labs originally planned to do the testing were dropped from the program.

Meacham cited a letter he had just obtained that was written by one of the labs' directors to the British Museum in January of this year, in which the current C-14 project was described as "a rather shoddy enterprise . . . which the British Museum may live to regret."

Meacham felt the matter could be easily clarified by another round of testing under proper controls, especially in view of the small amount of material needed to obtain a C-14 date. "We should have at least 5 or 6 dates on various points on the cloth before we can say anything definitive about its radiocarbon age," he said.[25]

In all the reports critical of the radiocarbon date, published on October 13 and October 14, 1988, there were signs of frustration, of the belief that something had gone wrong. No one, however, was able to pinpoint the problem. The date obtained for the Shroud by the three radiocarbon laboratories did not agree with the studies by Delage, Vignon, and Barbet. The reactions produced a negative environment that damaged true Shroud research.

LATE REACTIONS

Harry Gove, in his 1996 book, reported on an article, written by John Cornwall, that appeared in London in the newspaper *The Tablet* on January 14, 1989. The expert he interviewed "was asked how he thought the image was produced. He replied he personally thought it was the result of a scorch either done cleverly with a poker or as a bas relief using a heated statue. As for the blood, he said, who knew whether it was human or pig's blood?"[26]

Clyde Haberman, in the *New York Times* on Sunday June 11, 1989, had an article entitled "Despite Tests, Turin Shroud is Still Revered." He mentioned that eight months after the release of the radiocarbon-dating results, believers in the authenticity of the Shroud visit the Cathedral of Saint John the Baptist in Turin to revere the Shroud. He also wrote that English writer Ian Wilson had stated, "Until somebody can show me how the image was made . . . the carbon dating, for reasons we don't know, may be in error."[27]

Appendix F

THE TRUE CROSS

In Christian legend, all the trees of the forest rebelled at giving their wood for Jesus' Cross, except the holm oak. Yet Jesus forgave it because it was willing to die with him.

—MOLDENKE AND MOLDENKE[1]

RUCIFIXION WAS THE MOST SEVERE FORM OF PUNISH-ment used in ancient times. The Roman writer Cicero mentioned it as *"servile supplicium."* Before the Romans dominated Israel, the Hebrews did not practice crucifixion. The death penalty under their law was carried out by stoning. Only after Israel became a Roman province was crucifixion established in Palestine.

The Romans inflicted scourging on prisoners before they were crucified. After the revolt led by Spartacus, the Romans crucified six thousand slaves. Each condemned man had to carry the cross's horizontal bar, the patibulum, to the site of execution, where, entirely naked, he was nailed to that bar and then lifted to the vertical pole, the stipes. The patibulum usually had, in the middle, a mortise that could be inserted into the tenon in the stipes. In the Church of the

Santa Croce in Gerusalemme, in Lateran, Rome, is a patibulum believed to be from the cross of the Good Thief.

During the first century many persons died on the cross in Palestine. The Jewish historian Josephus, in *History of the Jewish Wars,* reported that Titus ordered the crucifixion of more than five hundred Jews a day in Jerusalem.[2] These numbers of crucifixions forced the Roman soldiers to produce the crosses from trees that were at hand and to make the procedure as simple as possible. The most common tree in Israel was the oak. In *The Shroud of Turin,* by Werner Bulst, S.J., the author wrote that the problem for making crosses in Jerusalem was that "lumber, even then, was unusually scarce in Palestine."[3]

The cross that the Romans preferred to use was the *crux commissa,* in the form of the Greek letter *tau.* Many Christian writers believe that Jesus of Nazareth was crucified on the *crux imissa,* also known as *crux capitata,* in which the stipes, the vertical post, extended above the patibulum and the upper part bore the inscription INRI, ordered by Pilate. The correct form of the crucifix of Jesus of Nazareth has not yet been proved, and I believe it never will be. If Jesus was crucified on a *crux immisa,* that indicates that the Romans made an exception in this instance.

TRUE CROSS

The city of Constantinople was consecrated on November 4, 328, by Emperor Constantine I. He erected four triumphal arches that supported a cupola, above which was the most venerable of the Christian relics, the True Cross. But how did this cross, come to be in the hands of the head of the Byzantine Empire?

The mother of Emperor Constantine I, Saint Helena, is said, by tradition, to have gone to Jerusalem in the year A.D. 326 to locate the remnants of the True Cross. With the help of Bishop Macarius, the patriarch of Jerusalem, Saint Helena located the area of the Holy Sepulcher and the three crosses buried in that site, near the Hill of Golgotha. In order to determine which of the three crosses was the one on which Jesus of Nazareth had been crucified, those seeking it used the body of a person who had recently died. When the dead body was placed on the wood of the True Cross, it immediately came back to life. The Church of the Holy Sepulcher was erected at the site where the three crosses were found.

It is interesting that Eusebius of Cesarea doesn't mention the finding of the True Cross in his *History of the Church* or in his *Life of Constantine.* The first person who reported the finding of the True Cross was Cyril of Jerusalem, in his book *Catechesis,* written in the year 348, twenty-two years after the apparent "invention" or "discovery" of the Holy Wood.[4]

The relic was kept in Jerusalem until, in the year 614, the Persian general Shahr-Baraz took Jerusalem and seized the True Cross, together with other relics. In 628, all the Jerusalem relics were recovered by the Byzantine Emperor Heraclius after his defeat of the Persians. On September 14 of that year Heraclius entered Constantinople in triumph. Norwich described the triumphal entrance:

> *The procession threaded its way slowly through the streets to St. Sophia, where Patriarch Sergius was waiting; and, at the solemn mass of thanksgiving that followed, the True Cross on which the Redeemer had died was slowly raised up until it stood, vertical, before the high altar.[5]*

In A.D. 629 Emperor Heraclius, his wife, Martina, and his older son, Constantine, returned the True Cross to Jerusalem.

> *On reaching the Holy City, he personally carried the Cross along the Via Dolorosa to the rebuilt Church of the Holy*

Sepulcher, where Patriarch Zacharias was waiting to receive
it back into his charge.[6]

Many portions of the Holy Wood were distributed to different
churches. Several segments are at St. Peter's Basilica in Rome, several
at the Holy Cross in Jerusalem at Lateran Rome. There are some in
Ravenna; in Vienna at the Cross of Charlemagne and the Cross of St.
Stephen; at Limburg, near Aachen, at the Cross of Victory. At the
cathedral in Cologne there are three reliquaries with segments of the
True Cross. Sections are in Milan at St. Mark's Cathedral, in the cathedral in Oviedo, and at Constantinople. A large segment of the True
Cross was sent by the Knights Templar in September 14, 1241, to
Saint Louis, King of France, who, barefooted, carried the Holy Wood
to the Saint Chapelle in Paris. In Segovia, Spain, at the Church of the
True Cross, which was a Templar temple, there are pieces. And many
other cathedrals contain segments of the True Cross.

WOODEN REMNANTS ON THE SHROUD

On the samples taken by Riggi on April 21, 1988, from the occipital
region of the Man on the Shroud were several blood smears that
contained some wooden remnants. I had the opportunity to study
two of them on the Scotch tape that was used by Riggi to peel the
blood from the Shroud. Each piece of tape was 2.0 cm by 0.5 cm, and
each removed several blood samples. The wood-related artifacts on
these two tapes were: (a) ten tubules of wood, (b) five wood fiber
groups, (c) a remnant of a leaf, (d) seven cleistothecia from fungi that
grow on wood.

The tubules of wood vessels on the Scotch tape vary in length
from 500 to 200 micrometers and in width from 250 to 120 micro-

meters, and they have the characteristic structure of tubules from oak *(Quercus)*. These tubules, which have become plasticized by the bacteria on the Shroud, are fragmented, and some of them are still embedded in blood. At present, it is not possible to determine the taxonomy of the wood fibers nor the leaf remnant, but they probably belong to oak, too.

With the optical microscope, I studied the anatomy of several species of oak, using histological thin sections and staining them with PAS in order to have a better idea of the tubules from different species of *Quercus,* but I have not yet been able to make a specific identification. Tradition indicates that the Cross was made of holm oak *(Quercus ilex)*. Until it is proved otherwise, I maintain that the remnants of wood found on the Shroud probably were splinters that had pierced the skin of the occipital region of the Man on the Shroud during the falls he suffered on his way to Golgotha.

The finding of the oak splinters mixed with the blood from the occipital region suggests that the horizontal beam of the Cross, the patibulum, was made of oak wood. Despite tradition, this finding is not in agreement with other microscopic studies of relics from the True Cross, which have been identified as pine.

There are four possible explanations of the discrepancy: (1) the patibulum was made of oak and the vertical beam, the stipes, was made of pine; (2) all the oak fragments in the blood of the occipital region are contaminants; (3) the Shroud of Turin is not the burial cloth of Jesus of Nazareth; (4) all the pine relics of the True Cross in all the churches, which have been venerated for seventeen hundred years, are fakes.

According to established tradition, the body of Jesus of Nazareth was taken from the Cross with the arms still nailed to the patibulum. The stipes was left in place to be used in other crucifixions. It is difficult to believe that a complete cross was discovered near Golgotha in A.D. 326.

CONCLUSION

The finding of the oak tubules, the wooden fibers, and the leaf remnants, mixed with the blood of the occipital region of the Man on the Shroud, indicates that the patibulum was not a neatly cut rectangular beam of pine but a rough oak log.

Notes
for Appendices

APPENDIX A. ANATOMY, BLOOD, AND DNA ON THE SHROUD

Part 1. Anatomy of the Man on the Shroud

1. Ian Wilson, *The Shroud of Turin: The Burial Cloth of Jesus Christ?*, 1978:82, front.
2. Manuel Sole, *La Sabana Santa de Turin*, 1984:205.
3. ———, 207.
4. ———, 210.
5. ———, 221.
6. ———, 234.
7. W. D. Edwards, W. J. Gabel, and F. E. Hosmer, "On the Physical Death of Jesus Christ," *Journal of the American Medical Association*, 1986:1456.
8. J. V. Klauder, *Stigmatization*, 1938:654.
9. ———, fn. 20.
10. ———, fn. 21.
11. W. D. Edwards, et al., *op. cit.*, 1458.
12. ———, 1459.
13. ———, 1458.
14. ———, 1462.
15. N. P. DePasquale and G. E. Burch, *Death by Crucifixion*, 1963:435.

16. S. M. Tenney, *On Death by Crucifixion*, 1964:286.

17. Giulio Ricci, *The Holy Shroud*, 1981:210.

18. John H. Heller, *Report on the Shroud of Turin*, 1983.

Part 2. Human Blood on the Shroud

1. W. C. McCrone and C. Skirius, "Light Microscopical Study of the Turin 'Shroud' I," *The Microscope*, 1980, 28:105–113.

2. ———II, 28:115–128.

3. ———, III, 29:19–38.

4. W. C. McCrone, "The Shroud of Turin: Blood or Artist's Pigment?" *Accounts of Chemical Research*, 1990, 23:77–83.

5. F. C. Neidhardt, J. L. Ingraham, and M. Schaechter, *Physiology of the Bacterial Cell: A Molecular Approach*, 1990:160.

Part 3. Human DNA on the Shroud. The DNA of God?

1. J. D. Watson, Michael Gilman, Jan Witkowski, and Mark Zoller, *Recombinant DNA*, 2nd ed., 1992:604.

2. Yutaka Nakahori, Osamu Takenaka, and Yasuo Nakagome, *A Human X-Y Homologus Region Encodes "Amelogenn,"* 1991:268.

APPENDIX B. A NATURALLY PLASTICIZED TEXTILE

Part 1. The Microbiology of the Shroud

1. Carl R. Woese, "There Must Be a Prokaryote Somewhere," *Microbiology's Search for Itself*, 1994:1.

2. A. Humbolt. In paper by W. E. Krumbein and K. Jens.

3. Ibid.

4. R. I. Dorn, *A Biological Model of Rock Varnish Formation*, 1980.

5. J. T. Staley, F. Palmer, and J. B. Adams, "Microcolonial Fungi: Common Inhabitants of Desert Rocks," *Science*, 213:1093–1094.

6. S. Taylor-George, et al., *Microbial Ecology* 1983, 9:227–245.

7. L. A. Garza-Valdes, *Biogenic Varnish on Ancient Pottery and Stone Artifacts*, 1993:52.

8. Carl R. Woese, *op. cit.*, 1994:6.

9. D. R. Caldwell, *Microbial Physiology and Metabolism*, 1995:20.

10. J. DeLey, *Comparative Carbohydrate Metabolism and a Proposal for a Phylogenetic Relationship of the Acetic Acid Bacteria,* 1961.

11. J. DeLey, J. Swings, and F. Gossele, *Acetobacter,* 1984.

12. M. Aschenr and J. Mager, *Synthesis of Cellulose by Resting Cells of Acetobacter xylinum,* 1947:64–65.

13. R. M. Brown, J.H.M. Willison, and C. L. Richardson, *Cellulose Biosynthesis in Acetobacter xylinum: Visualization of the Site of Synthesis and Direct Measurement of the in vivo Process,* 1976:4565–4569.

14. K. Zaar, *Visualization of Pores (export sites) Correlated with Cellulose Production in the Envelope of Gram-negative Bacterium Acetobacter xylinum,* 1979:773–777.

15. M. H. Deinema, L.P.T.M. Zevenhuizen, *Formation of cellulose fibrils by gram-negative bacteria and their role in Bacterial Flocculation,* 1971:42–57.

16. K. Kwon-Chung and J. Bennett, *Medical Mycology,* 1992:226.

17. P. J. VanDemark and B. L. Batzig, *The Microbes. An Introduction to Their Nature and Importance,* 1987:520.

18. *Bergey's Manual of Systemic Bacteriology,* vol I, 1984:311.

19. J. H. Heller, *op. cit.,* 1983:146.

20. B. J. Tindall, A. A. Mills, and W. D. Grant, *An Alkalophilic Red Halophilic Bacterium with a Low Magnesium Requirement from a Kenyan Soda Lake,* 1980:257–260.

21. B. J. Tindall, H.N.M. Ross, and W. D. Grant, *Natronobacterium gen. nov. and Natronococcus gen. nov. Two New Genera of Haloalkaliphilic Archaeobacteria,* 1984:41–57.

Part 2. A Naturally Plasticized Textile

1. Ian Wilson, *op. cit.,* 1978:8.

2. L. A. Garza-Valdes, *op. cit.,* 1983:55.

3. L. A. Garza-Valdes, "La Venta: The Mythical Tamoanchan," *Society for American Archaeology Abstracts,* 1984:56.

4. L. A. Garza-Valdes and G. R. Walters, "Chromium Chalcedony: The Mesoamerican Emerald," *Society for American Archaeology,* 1985.

5. E. G. Couzens, and V. E. Yarsley, *Plastics in a Modern World,* Penguin, Harmondsworth, Middlesex, 168:20.

6. Rosalie David, *Mysteries of the Mummies,* 1978:70.

7. ———, 1978:71.

8. ———, 1978:87.

9. ———, 1978:88.

10. ———, 1978:102.

11. ———, 1978:103.

12. ———, 1978:184.

13. H. E. Gove, S. J. Mattingly, A. R. David, and L. A. Garza-Valdes, *A Problematic Source of Organic Contamination of Linen*, 1997:504–507.

APPENDIX C. THE OFFICIAL SHROUD PHOTOGRAPHS

1. John Walsh, *The Shroud*, 1963:6.

2. *Ibid.*

3. ———, 1963:21.

4. ———, 1963:23.

5. ———, 1963:24.

6. ———, 1963:27.

7. ———, 1963:30.

8. *Ibid.*

9. ———, 1963:31.

10. *Ibid.*

11. U. Chevalier. *Le Saint Suaire de Turin, est-il l'original au une copie?*, 1899.

12. Edward A. Wuenschel, "The Holy Shroud. Present State of the Question," *American Ecclesiastical Review*, 1940, 102:465–486.

13. John Walsh, *op. cit.*, 1963:59.

14. ———, 1963:61.

15. Manuel Sole, *La Sabana Santa de Turin. Su autenticidad y Trascendencia*, 1984:34.

16. Kenneth E, Stevenson and Gary R. Habernas, *Verdict on the Shroud: Evidence for the Death and Resurrection of Jesus Christ*, 1981:57.

17. Ian Wilson, *op. cit.*, 1978:19.

18. ———, 1978:20.

19. John Walsh, *op. cit.*, 1963:126.

20. ———, 1963:129.

APPENDIX D. AN ACCELERATOR-BASED MASS SPECTROMETRY

The appendix was written by Dr. Harry E. Gove for inclusion in this book.

APPENDIX E. RADIOCARBON AND THE 1988 STUDY

1. H. E. Gove, *op. cit.*, 1996:7.
2. P. E. Damon et. al., *Radiocarbon dating of the Shroud of Turin*, 1989.
3. H. E. Gove, *op. cit.*, 1996:264.
4. ———, 1996:12.
5. ———, 1996:16.
6. Barbara J. Culliton, *The Mystery of the Shroud of Turin*, 1978.
7. *Ibid.*
8. H. E. Gove, *op. cit.*, 1996:144.
9. ———, 174.
10. ———, 215.
11. ———, 222.
12. ———, 230.
13. ———, 239.
14. ———, 245.
15. ———, 262.
16. ———, 266.
17. ———, 273.
18. ———, 277.
19. ———, 279.
20. ———, 280.
21. Orazio Petrosillo and E. Marinelli, *The Enigma of the Shroud: A Challenge to Science*, 1996:95.
22. ———, 93.
23. ———, 97.
24. ———, 105.
25. William Meacham, "Turin Shroud Dated to A.D. 200–1000 in Secret Testing: Results Inconsistent with Recent Dates," press release, University of Hong Kong, October 14, 1988.
26. H. E. Gove, op. cit., 1996:297.
27. ———, 304.

APPENDIX F. THE TRUE CROSS

1. H. N. Moldenke and A. L. Moldenke, *The Plants of the Bible,* 1952:199.

2. Flavius Josephus, *History of the Jewish War,* book V. chap. XI:1.

3. W. Bulst et al., *The Shroud of Turin,* Bruce Publishing Co., Milwaukee, 1957:45.

4. St. Cyril of Jerusalem, in *The Fathers of the Church, Catechesis.*

5. John J. Norwich, *Byzantium: The Early Centuries,* 1997:301.

6. ———, 305.

Bibliography

Aschenr, M. and J. Mager. "Synthesis of Cellulose by Resting Cells of Acetobacter Xylinum." Hebrew University, Jerusalem. *Nature*, 159:64–65, 1947.

Bailey, D. C. *Viva Cristo Rey! The Cristero Rebellion and the Church-State Conflict in Mexico.* University of Texas Press, Austin, 1974.

Barber, M. *The Trial of the Templars.* Cambridge University Press, 1978, Canto edition, paperback, 1993.

Barbet, P. *A Doctor at Calvary.* Doubleday, N.Y., 1953, Image books, 1963.

Beecher, P. A. *The Holy Shroud: Reply to the Rev. Herbert Thurston, S. J.* M. H. Gill and Son, Dublin, 1928.

Bergey's Manual of Systematic Bacteriology, 4 vols., Williams and Wilkins. Baltimore, MD, 1984–89.

Bowman, S. *Radiocarbon Dating.* University of California Press, Berkeley, 1990.

Brinkman, F. CSSR. "The Theory of Image Formation of the Holy Shroud of Turin as Proposed by Dr. Leoncio A. Garza-Valdes," *Holy Shroud Guild News Letter,* Bronx, NY, 1993.

Brown, R. M., J. H. M. Willison and C. L. Richardson. "Cellulose Biosynthesis in *Acetobacter xylinum:* Visualization of the Site of Synthesis and Direct Measurement of the *In Vivo* Process," Procedures of the National Academy of Sciences, 1976, 73:4565–4569.

Bucklin, R. *The Medical Aspects of the Crucifixion of Christ.* Sindon, 7:5–11, 1961.

Bulst, W., S. McKeena and J. J. Galvin. *The Shroud of Turin.* Bruce Publishing Co., Milwaukee, 1957.

Burman, E. *The Templars: Knights of God.* Destiny Books. Rochester, VT, 1986.

Byron, D. "Polyhydroxyalkanoates," *Plastics from Microbes, Microbial Synthesis of Polymers and Polymer Precursors,* D. P. Mobley, ed., Hanser Publications. Cincinnati, 1994.

Caldwell, D. R. *Microbial Physiology and Metabolism.* Wm. C. Brown Publishers, Dubuque, IA, 1995.

Carreno-Etxeandia, J. L., SDB. *La Sabana Santa.* 2nd ed. Ediciones Don Bosco, Mexico, 1988.

Chevalier, U. *Le Saint Suaire de Turin, Est-il L'original ou Une Copie?* Menard, Chambery, 1899.

———. *Étude Critique sur L'origine du S. Suaire de Lirey-Chambery-Turin.* A. Picard, Paris, 1900.

———. *Le Saint Suaire de Turin: Historie d'une Relique.* A. Picard, Paris, 1902.

Chrétien de Troyes. *Percival, or the Story of the Grail.* Translated by Ruth Harwood Cline. University of Georgia Press. Athens, Georgia, 1985.

Culliton, Barbara J. "The Mystery of the Shroud of Turin." *Science,* 1978.

Currer-Briggs, N. *The Shroud and the Grail: A Modern Quest for the True Grail.* Weidenfield and Nicholson, London, 1987.

Cyril of Jerusalem. *The Fathers of the Church. St. Cyril of Jerusalem,* vol 64. The Catholic University of America Press, Washington, DC, 1970.

Damon, P. E., D. J. Donahue, B. H. Gore, A. L. Hathaway, A.J.T. Jull, T. W. Linick, P. J. Sercel, L. J. Toolin, C. R. Bronk, E. T. Hall, R.E.M. Hedges, R. Housley, I. A. Law, C. Perry, G. Bonani, S. Trumbore, W. Woelfli, J. C. Ambers, S.G.E. Bowman, M. N. Leese, and M. S. Tite. "Radiocarbon Dating of the Shroud of Turin," *Nature,* 337:611–615, 1989.

David, R. *Mysteries of the Mummies: The Story of the Unwrapping of a 2000-Year-old Mummy by a Team of Experts.* Charles Scribner's Sons, New York, 1978.

Deinema, M. H. and L.P.T.M. Zevenhuizen. "Formation of Cellulose Fibrils by Gram-negative Bacteria and Their Role in Bacterial Flocculation," *Archives of Microbiology,* 78:42–57, 1971.

Delage, Yves. "Le Linceul de Turin." *Révue Scientifique,* 4 ser., 17:683–687, 1902.

De Ley, Jozef. "Comparative Carbohydrate Metabolism and a Proposal for a Phylogenetic Relationship of the Acetic Acid Bacteria." *Journal of General Microbiology*, 24:31–50, 1961.

De Ley, J., J. Swings, and F. Gossele. "Acetobacter." *Bergey's Manual of Systematic Bacteriology*, 1:268–274, 1984.

DePasquale, N. P. and G. E. Burch. "Death by Crucifixion." *American Heart Journal*, 66:434–435, 1963.

Dorn, R. I. "A Biological Model of Rock Varnish Formation." *Abstracts*. Pacific Division, American Association for the Advancement of Science. University of California, Davis, 50, 1980.

Edwards, W. D., W. J. Gabel, and F. E. Hosmer. "On the Physical Death of Jesus Christ," *Journal of the American Medical Association*, 255:1455–1463, 1986.

Frei, M. "Nine Years of Palynological Studies on the Shroud." *Shroud Spectrum International*, 3:3–7, 1982.

Garza-Valdes, L. A. "Specific Iconography of Olmec Rulers." Annual Meeting, Society for American Archaeology. Pittsburg, PA., *Abstracts*, 48:55, 1983.

———. "La Venta, the Mythical Tamoanchan." Annual Meeting, Society for American Archaeology. Portland, OR., *Abstracts*, 48:55, 1984.

———. "Opal Deposits on Maya Artifacts." II Maya Symposium, Austin, TX., *Abstracts*, 1986.

———. "Technology and Weathering of Mesoamerican Jades as Guides to Authenticity." Materials Research Society Symposium Proceedings, *Materials Issues in Art and Archaeology*, II. P. B. Vandiver, J. R. Druzik and G. Wheeler, eds., 185:321–357, 1991.

———. "Human Blood on a Pre-Columbian Celt (The Itzamna Tun)." 28th International Symposium on Archaeometry, Los Angeles, CA., *Archaeometry*, 92:18, 1992b.

———. "Biogenic Varnish on Ancient Pottery and Stone Artifacts." Society For American Archaeology, 58th Annual Meeting, St. Louis, MO., *Abstracts*, 58:52, 1993a.

———. "Mesoamerican Jade, Surface Changes Caused by Natural Weathering." *Pre-Columbian Jade, New Geological and Cultural Interpretations*, ed. F. W. Lange, University of Utah Press, 104–124, 1993b.

———. "Lichenothelia Varnish and the Shroud of Turin." Summary. Rome, Italy. June 11, 1993. *Holy Shroud Guild News Letter*, Bronx, NY. July 1993, 1993c.

Garza-Valdes, L. A. and T. R. Hester. "Maya Green Stone Artifacts: Instrumental Analysis." *Program and Abstracts*. Scientific Perspectives on the Problem of Art and Artifact Origins. University of Texas at San Antonio. San Antonio, TX, 1987.

Garza-Valdes, L. A., G. Riggi di Numana, E. K. Eskew, V. V. Tryon, and S. J. Mattingly. "Microbial Analysis of the Shroud of Turin and Its Potential Effect on the Interpretation of the Previous Radiocarbon Dating." 95th General Meeting. Society for American Microbiology, *Abstracts,* Washington, DC.

Garza-Valdes, L. A. and B. Stross. "Rock Varnish on a Pre-Columbian Green Jasper from the Tropical Rain Forest (The Ahaw Pectoral)." Materials Research Society Symposium, *Proceedings. Materials Issues in Art and Archaeology,* III. P. B. Vandiver, J. R. Druzik, G. Wheeler, and I. C. Freestone, eds. 267:891–900, 1992.

Garza-Valdes, L. A. and G. R. Walters. "Chromium Chalcedony: The Mesoamerican Emerald." 50th Annual Meeting. Society for American Archaeology, *Abstracts,* Denver, 1985.

Garza-Valdes, L. A., T. S. Widish, P. Hoffman, and S. J. Mattingly. "Filamentous Fungi on the Shroud of Turin." 96th General Meeting, American Society of Microbiology. *Abstracts,* New Orleans, LA., 1996.

Gilliland, R. and J. P. Lacey. "Lethal Action by an Acetobacter on Yeasts." *Nature,* 202:727–728, 1964.

Glazer, A. N. and H. Nikaido. *Microbial Biotechnology: Fundamentals of Applied Microbiology*. W. H. Freeman and Co., New York, 1995.

Goodrich, N. L. *The Holy Grail.* Harper Perennial ed., NY, 1992.

Gove, H. E. *Relic, Icon or Hoax? Carbon Dating the Turin Shroud.* Institute of Physics Publishers. Bristol, U.K., 1996.

Gove, H. E., S. J. Mattingly, A. R. David, and L. A. Garza-Valdes. "A Problematic Source of Organic Contamination of Linen." *Nuclear Instruments and Methods in Physics, Research B,* 123:504–507, 1997.

Heller, J. H. *Report on the Shroud of Turin.* Houghton Mifflin Co., Boston, MA., 1983.

Heller, J. H. and A. Adler "Blood on the Shroud of Turin." *Applied Optics,* 19:2742–2744, 1980.

Jackson, J., E. Jumper, W. Mottern, and K. Stevenson. "The Three-Dimensional Image on Jesus' Burial Cloth." *Proceedings of the 1977 United States Conference of Research on the Shroud of Turin.* March 23–24, 1977. Albuquerque, New Mexico. Holy Shroud Guild, Bronx, NY, 74–94, 1977.

The Jerusalem Bible. Doubleday, NY., 1966.

Josephus, F. *The Complete Works of Josephus.* Kregel Publications, Grand Rapids, Michigan, 565, 1981.

Jumper, E. J., A. D. Adler, J. P. Jackson, S. F. Pellicori, J. H. Heller, and J. R. Druzik. "A Comprehensive Examination of the Various Stains and Images on the Shroud of Turin," *Archaeological Chemistry,* III. J. B. Lambert, ed., *Advances in Chemistry,* no. 205 American Chemical Society, 1984.

Klauder, J. V. "Stigmatization." *Archives Dermatology Syphilology,* 37:650–659, 1938.

Knauss, K. G. and T. L. Ku. "Desert Varnish: Potential for Age Dating via Uranium-Series Isotopes." *Journal Geology,* 88:95–100, 1980.

Krumbein, W. E. and K. Jens. "Biogenic Rock Varnishes on the Negev Desert (Israel): An Ecological Study of Iron and Manganese Transformation by Cyanobacteria and Fungi." *Oecologia,* 50:26, 1981.

Kwon-Chung, K. and J. E. Bennett, *Medical Mycology.* Lea and Febiger. Malvern, PA, 1992.

Lemoigne, M. "Produits de Deshydratation et de Polymerisation de L'acide Beta Oxybutyrique." *Bull. Soc. Chim. Biol.* 8:770–781, 1926.

Lockhart, R. D., G. F. Hamilton, and F. W. Fyfe. *Anatomy of the Human Body.* Faber and Faber, Ltd. London, 1959.

Loomis, R. S. *The Grail: From Celtic Myth to Christian Symbol.* Princeton University Press. Princeton, NJ., 1991.

McCrone, W. C. "Light Microscopical Study of the Turin Shroud," II. *Microscope,* 28:115–128, 1980.

———. "Microscopical Study of the Turin 'Shroud,' " III. *Microscope,* 29:19–38, 1981.

——— "The Shroud of Turin: Blood or Artist's Pigment?" *Accounts of Chemical Research,* 23:77–83, 1990.

McCrone, W. C. and C. Skirius. "Light Microscopical Study of the Turin Shroud," I. *Microscope,* 28:105–113, 1980.

McDowell, B., with photographs by J. L. Stanfield. *Inside the Vatican.* National Geographic Society, Washington, DC., 1991.

Miller, J. Michael. "The Encyclicals of John Paul II." *Our Sunday Visitor Publishing, Inc.,* Huntington, IN., 1996.

Moldenke, H. N. and A. L. Moldenke. *Plants of the Bible.* Dover Publications, Mineola NY, 1952.

Nakahori, Y., K. Hamano, M. Iwaya, and Y. Nakagome. "Sex Identification by Polymerase Chain Reaction Using X–Y Homologous Primer." *American Journal of Medical Genetics,* 39:472–473, 1991.

Nakahori, Y., O. Takenaka, and Y. Nakagome. "A Human X–Y Homologous Region Encodes 'Amelogenin.'" *Genomics*, 9:264–269, 1991.

Neidhardt, F. C., J. L. Ingrahamn, and M. Schaechter. *Physiology of the Bacterial Cell: A Molecular Approach*. Sinauer Associated, Inc., Sunderland, MA, 1990.

Norwich, John Julius. *Byzantium: The Early Centuries*. Alfred A. Knopf. NY, 1997.

O'Connell, P. and C. Carty. *The Holy Shroud and Four Visions: A Reply to the Parisian Surgeon Pierre Barbet, M.D., Author of* A Doctor at Calvary. Tan Books and Publishers, Inc. Rockford, IL., 1974.

Pernoud, R. *Joan of Arc: By Herself and Her Witnesses*. Scarborough House, Lanham, MD, 1982.

Petrosillo, O. and E. Marinelli. *The Enigma of the Shroud: A Challenge to Science*. Publishers Enterprises Group (PEG), Malta, 1996.

Piperno, D. R. *Phytolith Analysis: An Archaeological and Geological Perspective*. Academic Press, San Diego, CA, 1988.

Ricci, Giulio. *The Holy Shroud*. Center for the Study of the Passion of Christ and the Holy Shroud. Milwaukee, WI, 1981.

Riggi di Numana, G. *Rapporto Sindone 1978–1982*. 3m edizioni. Il Piccolo Editore, Torino, 165, 1988.

Riley-Smith. *The Crusades: A Short History*. Yale University Press, New Haven, CT, 1987.

Sasikala, C. and C. V. Ramana. "Biotechnological Potentials of Anoxygenic Phototrophic Bacteria, II. Biopolyesters, Biopesticide, Biofuel, and Biofertilizer." *Advances in Applied Microbiology*. Academic Press., 41:227–278, 1991.

Sole, Manuel, S.J. *La Sabana Santa de Turin. Su Autenticidad y Trascendencia*. Ediciones Mensajero, Bilbao, Spain, 1984.

Staley, J. T., F. E. Palmer, and J. B. Adams. "Microcolonial Fungi: Common Inhabitants of Desert Rocks." *Science*, 213:1093–1094, 1982.

Stevenson, K. and G. Habermas. *Verdict on the Shroud*. Servant, Ann Arbor, MI, 1981.

Stross, B. and L. A. Garza-Valdes. "The Shamanic Fire of Maya Creation." Manuscript on file, Anthropology Department, University of Texas, Austin, 1992.

———. "Gems and the Maya Shaman." Manuscript on file, Anthropology Department, University of Texas, Austin, 1993.

Taylor-George, S., F. Palmer, J. T. Staley, D. J. Borns, B. Curtiss, and J. B.

Adams. "Fungi and Bacteria Involved in Desert Varnish Formation." *Microbial Ecology*, 9:227–245, 1983.

Tenney, S. M. "On Death by Crucifixion." *American Heart Journal*, 68:286–287, 1964.

Thurston, H. "The Holy Shroud and the Verdict of History." *The Month*, 101:17–29, 1903a.

———. "The Holy Shroud as a Scientific Problem." *The Month*, 101:162–178, 1903b.

Tindall, B. J., A. A. Mills, and W. D. Grant. "An Alkalophilic Red Halophilic Bacterium with a Low Magnesium Requirement from a Kenyan Soda Lake." *Journal of General Microbiology*, 116:257–260, 1980.

Tindall, B. J., H.N.M. Ross, and W. D. Grant. "Natronobacterium Gen. Nov. and Natronococcus Gen. Nov. Two New Genera of Haloalkaliphilic Archaebacteria." *System. Appl. Microbiol.*, 5:41–57, 1984.

Tonelli, Antonio. *La Santa Sindone. Esame Oggetivo*. Societa Editice Internazionale, Torino, 1931.

Twain, M. *Personal Recollections of Joan of Arc*. Random House, repr. 1995.

VanDemark, P. J. and B. L. Batzig. *The Microbes: An Introduction to Their Nature and Importance*. The Benjamin/Cummings Publishing Co. Inc., Reading, MA, 1987.

Vignon, Paul. *The Shroud of Christ*. trans. from the French, 1902 ed., E. P. Dutton, New York.

———. *Le Saint-Suaire de Turin Devant la Science, l'Archeologie, l'Histoire, l'Iconographie, la Logique*. Masson et Cie. 2 ed., Paris, 1939.

Walsh, J. *The Shroud*. Random House, NY, 1963.

Watson, J. D., M. Gilman, J. Witkowski, and M. Zoller. *Recombinant DNA*. 2nd ed., Scientific American Books, W. H. Freeman and Co., NY, 1992.

Wilcox, R. K. *Shroud*, Macmillan, NY, 1977.

Wilson, I. *The Shroud of Turin: The Burial Cloth of Jesus Christ?* Doubleday, Garden City, NY, 1978.

Wilson, I. and V. Miller. *The Mysterious Shroud*. Doubleday, Garden City, NY, 1986.

Woese, C. R. "There Must Be a Prokaryote Somewhere: Microbiology's Search for Itself." *Microbiological Reviews*, 58:1–9, 1994.

Wuenschel, E. A. "The Holy Shroud: Present State of the Question." *American Ecclesiastical Review*. 102:465–485, 1940.

———. *Self-Portrait of Christ: The Holy Shroud of Turin.* Holy Shroud Guild. Esopus, New York, 1954.

Zaar, K. "Visualization of Pores (Export Sites) Correlated with Cellulose Production in the Envelope of Gram-negative Bacterium Acetobacter Xylinum." *Journal of Cellular Biology,* 80:773–777, 1979.

DR. LEONCIO A. GARZA-VALDES
ROSA VERDE TOWER
343 W. HOUSTON ST. SUITE 612
SAN ANTONIO, TX 78205
U.S.A.
PHONE: (210) 223-2811
FAX: (210) 223-4105
E-MAIL: LAGARZAV@FLASH.NET